ARCO
Literary Critiques

Fielding

Hamilton Macallister

arco
New York

Published 1971 by ARCO PUBLISHING COMPANY, Inc.
219 Park Avenue South, New York, N.Y. 10003
Copyright © Hamilton Macallister, 1967,
All Rights Reserved
Library of Congress Catalog Number 70-123551
Printed in the United States of America

Arco Literary Critiques

Of recent years, the ordinary man who reads for pleasure has been gradually excluded from that great debate in which every intelligent reader of the classics takes part. There are two reasons for this: first, so much criticism floods from the world's presses that no one but a scholar living entirely among books can hope to read it all; and second, the critics and analysts, mostly academics, use a language that only their fellows in the same discipline can understand.

Consequently criticism, which should be as 'inevitable as breathing'—an activity for which we are all qualified—has become the private field of a few warring factions who shout their unintelligible battle cries to each other but make little communication to the common man.

Arco Literary Critiques aims at giving a straightforward account of literature and of writers—straightforward both in content and in language. Critical jargon is as far as possible avoided; any terms that must be used are explained simply; and the constant preoccupation of the authors of the Series is to be lucid.

It is our hope that each book will be easily understood, that it will adequately describe its subject without pretentiousness so that the intelligent reader who wants to know about Donne or Keats or Shakespeare will find enough in it to bring him up to date on critical estimates.

Even those who are well read, we believe, can benefit from a lucid exposition of what they may have taken for granted, and perhaps—dare it be said?—not fully understood.

K. H. G.

Fielding

The reputation of the 'father of the English novel' has suffered because he had a strong personality. We can't get away from Hogarth's drawing of him; for one thing it is the only authentic likeness. Furthermore, Fielding's letters and personal effects were burnt in the Gordon Riots of 1780. This may have been a good thing; Fielding, though he is a ripe subject for it, is saved from the sort of punishing biography that is fashionable nowadays. On the other hand I think it is a pity that there is no biography of him at this moment in print in England, and no collected edition of the prose works that are still widely read. As for the rest—nine-tenths of his output and some of it quite lively reading—it lies buried in ancient editions, consigned apparently to oblivion. *Shamela*, now that it is known to be Fielding's, ought to be included with any unabridged edition of *Joseph Andrews*. I think Fielding is worth discovering, and I would like to thank Kenneth Grose for suggesting this book, and for many helpful comments.

H. M.

Contents

The Author

Hamilton Macallister, M.A., is Senior English Master at Leiston Grammar School, East Suffolk, and is the author of two novels, *The Gilded Fly* and *The Marvellous Boy*.

'Adams's visit to Parson Trulliber' by Cruikshank (see *Joseph Andrews*, II, 14)

'Tom Jones and the landlord, Partridge and Susan, Mrs. Waters and the landlady' by Rowlandson (see *Tom Jones*, IX, 3)

'Print of a Winter's Morning', after the drawing by Hogarth
(see *Tom Jones* I, 11)

'Blear-eyed Moll' by Cruikshank (see *Amelia*, I, ·3)

I

Fielding's Reputation

Henry Fielding was born in 1707 and died in 1754. In his lifetime he was attacked, dismissed as contemptible, and praised, but generally the praise came later. By the turn of the century he was one of the masters; Gibbon said he would survive the 'Imperial Eagle of the House of Austria'—this being a reference to the mistaken belief that Fielding was descended from the Hapsburgs. Coleridge said the plot of *Tom Jones* was one of the three 'most perfect' ever planned, the other two being those of Ben Jonson's *The Alchemist* and Sophocles's *Oedipus Tyrannus*. In Thackeray's opinion Fielding was the last novelist 'to be able to describe a man'. During this time abuse continued, but of a sort that suggested always that Fielding had made an impact. Doctor Johnson had described him as a 'blockhead':

> Fielding being mentioned, Johnson exclaimed, 'he was a blockhead;' and upon my expressing my astonishment at so strange an assertion, he said, 'What I mean by his being a blockhead is that he was a barren rascal.' BOSWELL'S LIFE OF JOHNSON
> Oxford Ed., p. 480

'Who,' asked Doctor Burney, 'would venture to read one of Fielding's novels aloud to modest women?' He was called 'Ostler' by Richardson, who certainly had reason for disliking Fielding; 'Disgusting', from de Quincey; 'Stoops to carrion', from Charlotte Brontë, and so on. But in the early years of this century George Saintsbury classed him with Shakespeare, Milton and Swift: 'the four Atlantes'. Saintsbury wrote of him in 1912, '. . . if he has sometimes been equalled, [Fielding] has never been surpassed; and it is not easy to see how he can be surpassed'.

The word 'disgusting' is no longer now a term of literary abuse, and we don't go in for 'modest women' any longer. But in the years after the First World War Fielding's reputation suffered severely. Dr. F. R. Leavis summed up the case against him in 1948, when he said, 'There can't be subtlety of organisation without richer matter to organise, and subtler interests, than Fielding has to offer.' Twelve years earlier David Garnett had written as follows:

> His characters never rise above the obvious; there is no such thing as idealism or poetry, or romantic frenzy, or the stark staring lunacy which play so important a part in human affairs. Fielding can be sentimental, but he can never be idealistic. Because he had observed that people act with self-interest, he inclines to believe that their motives are always self-interested too.
>
> THE ENGLISH NOVELISTS

V. S. Pritchett, summarising the popular case against Fielding in 1946 in his book, *The Living Novel*, said his cult had passed with the 'masculine' tradition of the 'muscular Christians'; Fielding is accused of being a 'man's man', whose world 'turns out to be a box of tricks'; 'hearty . . . towny . . . insensitive'.

I think if we want to look for reasons for this swing away from Fielding, we must look to the novel itself, in the first quarter of this century. Fielding, rather than Richardson, his contemporary, was hailed as the 'father of the English novel', a strain that runs through Austen, Scott, Dickens, Thackeray, Eliot, Wells, Bennett, towards modern writers like J. B. Priestley. In the words of Leavis: 'He is important not because he leads to Mr. J. B. Priestley but because he leads to Jane Austen, to appreciate whose distinction is to feel that life isn't long enough to permit of one's giving much time to Fielding or any to Mr. Priestley.' Fielding's descendants are no longer central to the modern novel. He went out, V. S. Pritchett said, with 'the cult of the psychological novel'. In 1954 *The Times Literary Supplement* marked the bicentenary of Fielding's death with more of that peculiarly damning criticism that often goes with faint praise, to which was added a common modern reaction to Fielding: that he is smug. The modern reader, it suggested, likes his irony to be more 'ambivalent': 'a smug ... presumption of virtuous superiority ... infects the tone' of Fielding's work.

But since then I think there has been a change of feeling towards the novel in general, and towards Fielding. As far as Fielding is concerned, in England, we might pin-point the change to a defence of him against *The Times* criticisms by J. Middleton Murry, later published in his *Unprofessional Essays*. Murry said Fielding stood for love; not just *eros* (sexual love), but *agape* (brotherly love); and he praised Fielding's nobility of mind. (A curious thing about Fielding is the warmth and enthusiasm of his admirers; there is very little dispassionate praise of him.) Several studies of the novels and of Fielding's thought have recently come from America. It may be, from the point of view of the 20th century, that there is something distinctly American about him; America took its Constitution from the political ideas of Locke, and its way of life from 18th-century England, and Locke, along with the lesser-known third Earl of Shaftesbury, influenced Fielding widely. And along with this the novel has been changing. In one of Kingsley Amis's novels, *I Like it Here*, his hero visits Fielding's grave in Portugal and pays tribute to him. Whether or not the 'provincial' novel, which started off in the 1950s with works like Amis's *Lucky Jim*, turns out to be a fruitful development, I think that Fielding has an affinity with modern English writers of this type—one detail, for example, of a sort that can be significant: Amis, like Fielding, refers to his hero habitually by his surname. And Fielding has an affinity with the modern American novelists, who try, one after the other, to write about society as a whole, often with the 'epic' ambition which Fielding had. Fielding had the 'gregarious rather than the single eye' (V. S. Pritchett); he was interested in a man's views, his religion, philosophy and all the external things that put him in society.

The aim of this study is not to bulldoze the reader into accepting any valuation of Fielding. The five prose works, of which two are widely known, and the one play still in circulation, will have to speak for themselves. M. C. Battestin, in his book *The*

Moral Basis of Fielding's Art, quotes from a minor work long forgotten, a 'Gothic' fantasy called *A Journey from this World to the
Next,* in which Fielding imagines Minos standing guard at the
entrance to Elysium: 'No man,' he says, 'enters that gate without
charity.' Charity is the key to Fielding, at the centre of his
philosophy and religion. Minos rejects a succession of applicants
of the sort one meets repeatedly in the novels: two would-be
philosophers, an example of the worst type of contemporary
'latitudinarian' parson, a coquette and a prude. But he admits the
narrator, who is obviously Fielding:

> The judge then addressed himself to me, who little expected to pass
> this fiery trial. I confessed I had indulged myself very freely with
> wine and women in my youth, but had never done an injury to any
> man living, nor avoided an opportunity of doing good, that I
> pretended to very little virtue more than general philanthropy and
> private friendship.—I was proceeding when Minos bid me enter,
> and not indulge myself with trumpeting forth my virtues.
>
> THE COMPLETE WORKS II, 244
Ed. HENLEY

This is not a bad, short biography of Fielding, though you can
see features of the style that might irritate some people; it is self-
conscious, 'polished' in the manner of the 18th century, and
the deprecatory note struck in the last few words, designed to
take away the effect of the earlier self-praise, is carefully contrived; to some this might give an impression of smugness. If
you know about it, the tragedy and heroism of Fielding's
personal life tend to diminish the smugness, I think.

Is the modern novel moving back to Fielding? Probably there
are features of his work—his strong, fatalistic belief in Providence,
for example—that prevent Fielding from appealing much to the
moderns. Saintsbury admitted there was no mystery in Fielding;
he belongs 'to the light of day'. 'Dogmatically, then,' Wyndham
Lewis said, 'I am for the Great Without, for the method of the
external approach.' No writer was more 'external' in his methods
than Fielding; the characters are all kept at a distance, and he,
Fielding, sitting in his 'little parlour' as he calls it in *Tom Jones,*
is the one character close to the reader. It seems as if you can't

have this approach and sensitivity too; at least not the kind of sensitivity Elizabeth Bowen had in mind when she said the novel was like a 'non-poetic statement of a poetic truth'. The novel sways back and forth between these two approaches. 'Literature must always represent a battle between real people and images,' the novelist Iris Murdoch wrote in 1961, 'and what is required now is a much stronger and more complex conception of the former.' Like his friend Hogarth, the artist, Fielding was for 'real people' in the literary battle between real people and images.

Dr. Leavis had said in 1948 that the great English novelists 'are all distinguished by a vital capacity for experience, a kind of reverent openness before life, and a marked moral intensity'. I think, though, that we could go from that to an essay published in 1966 by Lionel Trilling in which he says of Leavis, '. . . he does not give anything like adequate recognition to those aspects of art which are gratuitous, which rise from high spirits and an impulse to play'. Fielding gains from a trend in this direction. Today, I think he would be granted moral intensity. He is irreverent; he puts up a philistine front. In one of his flippant, essay-type chapters that introduce the books of *Tom Jones*, and which readers tend to skip, he says, speaking of books on the 'marvellous': 'a horse-laugh in the reader would (not) be any great prejudice or mortification'. The horse-laugh puts people off; one has to get past it to the real Fielding.

2

The Background

Fielding's canvas was the whole of society. His writings are full of religious, philosophical and political ideas, though his main theme in his own words (see *Tom Jones*) was 'human nature'. So one could well come to him from a study of the whole period. For that, see the bibliography; but I am going to try to sum up here the features of his age that one sees in his novels.

It was an age that has lent itself to generalisations. The Age of Elegance, the Age of Reason, the Augustan Age, the Age of Enlightenment: the civil and religious strife of the previous century had given way after 1688 to a period of open discussion, reaction against intolerance, faith in man; in fact life in this country assumed a recognisably modern pattern at about this time. The political and religious compromises were made that have persisted, though politically it was a confused period, and toleration did not include the Roman Catholics.

But one could argue. It was the time when it was thought that one could reason one's way into Christianity. We see this confidence in reason and confidence in Christianity (of the 18th-century kind) coming together, for example, in Pope's *Essay on Man*. It produced a peculiar kind of superficial optimism, which hadn't existed before and would never exist again. Before this time there wasn't the faith in reason (it was faith, rather than reason); after it there was never again quite the same faith in Christianity. The Christian in future was not to look to his reasoning powers to reinforce his faith; instead he tended to put his reason and his faith in separate compartments.

But for a time, reason was thought to be the instrument that would solve all problems. In the days after the Glorious Revolution of 1688, when James II was driven from England, and before the French Revolution of 1789, there was a calm certainty, for most people, about the basic things of life. It was a good time for optimists, though what could not be put to the test of argument, the things of the spirit, were undervalued. Anything that could not be explained was undervalued; this was not a good time for lyrical poetry. But with the new curiosity about life came a curiosity about day-to-day life, and here the novel began.

It began when writers were no longer content to examine what Johnson, in the words of Imlac from his novel *Rasselas* (1759), called 'not the individual, but the species'. The poet, Johnson said, 'does not number the streaks of the tulip, or describe the different shades of the verdure of the forest'. The poet didn't, and that was why *Rasselas* and the early novels of that type are almost unreadable today. Johnson, when he said that, had forgotten Shakespeare, who was always concerned with particular people, and the detail of life, and so were the new novelists. Richardson, notably, described the streaks of every tulip he encountered, and his first novel, *Pamela* (1740), was the immediate cause of Fielding's *Joseph Andrews*, published two years later.

With these two we have what is generally regarded as the birth of the novel. *Pamela* was the first popular best-seller, and *Joseph Andrews*, though more closely anchored to the past, to the theatre, and to an older type of characterisation than was *Pamela* (Fielding said himself in words that anticipate Johnson that he was describing 'species', not individuals), was probably the first English novel of major importance. V. S. Pritchett said of Fielding that we often seem, when reading him, to have met it all before; and that is because so many later English novelists, such as Dickens and Thackeray, took over some of his material, repeated it and developed it.

These early novels by Fielding and Richardson were, as the word implies, 'news': news about life. Defoe had prepared the way with his sober descriptions of day-to-day life in *Robinson Crusoe* (1719) and *A Journal of the Plague Year* (1722). To Defoe the streaks of the tulip were always important. There were many

15

novels before this time but they were not about real people against a realistic setting; mostly they did not have the names of real people. Euphues, Badman, Chloë—where they had the Christian names of real people, they tended not to have surnames. The new novels, on the other hand, were more conscious than the plays or poetry of the past of the passage of time. In Richardson's long epistolary novels every hour had to be accounted for; Fielding in *Tom Jones* tells us with careful accuracy how much time has passed or is to be covered. Hazlitt said of Richardson, '. . . he set about describing every object and transaction, as if the whole had been given as evidence by an eye-witness'. Lamb said of Defoe, '. . . it is like reading evidence in a court of justice'. Addison, in his *Spectator*, one of the first daily journals, made his characters speak 'ordinary conversation'. It is in the journalistic writings of Steele and Addison, in the *Tatler* and the later *Spectator*, in the creation of characters such as Addison's Sir Roger de Coverley, that we see the beginnings of this new form of writing. You can take it further back—to Petronius's *Satyricon* of the 1st century A.D., if you like. But here, in Steele and Addison, was a new interest in ordinary life, what a man did in his spare time, quiet hours in country houses. Falstaff we see at certain moments; Sir Roger de Coverley we get to know more thoroughly. Richardson's Pamela, Clarissa—there is very little we don't know about the lives of these women, by the time he has finished with them. Along with this consider the new prosperity of the middle class, which made a 'public' possible, instead of aristocratic patronage, and the invention of circulating libraries (the first one in London dates from 1741) and we see conditions ripe for the modern novel. It burst upon us suddenly with four writers; Richardson (1689–1761), a middle-aged book-seller, who influenced Proust and all women's magazine fiction; Fielding (1707–1754), who set the distinctive shape of the English novel, theatrical, picaresque, a loose, complex plot holding together a great variety of material; Smollett (1721–1771), who developed a distinctively English fictional 'character', the caricature which Dickens developed into his grotesque fantasies; and Sterne (1713–1768), who took the new preoccupation with minutiae, with the detail of life, as far as anyone has taken it. It has been pointed out that every conceivable kind of novel, from James Joyce to Virginia Woolf to C. P. Snow, can find some ancestry in these four writers.

IDEAS AND BELIEFS

Fielding was not one of the English 'Augustans'—so called from their fancied affinity with the 'golden age' of Roman literature, the reign of the emperor Augustus under which Virgil, Horace and Ovid flourished. Fielding came between periods; Addison died in 1719 when Fielding was twelve, and Swift and Pope, the great English Augustans, did not survive long after 1742, when Fielding's first novel was published.

But Fielding had many of the traits of the Augustans. This was a period when writers generally took more part in public life than they had done before or have done since. They were highly regarded and influential. It was a time when writers thought of themselves as part of the community and the community acclaimed them—Pope, for example, got £6,000 for his translation of Homer. Philosophic ideas, particularly those of Locke, were eagerly discussed by everyone, and Shakespeare and Milton were universally admired and read, without the competition which they faced later from masses of ephemeral literature. Richardson's Pamela read Locke rather as a modern housewife and mother reads Doctor Spock.

There was a filtering process. The most difficult of the philosophers and the most pessimistic, Thomas Hobbes (1588–1679), was amended, his uncompromising views modified, by Locke. John Locke (1632–1704) was a conformist, and had the good luck to have opinions which were well timed politically. England after the Revolution of 1688 was ready for his tolerant conservatism. The Stuarts had been got rid of and before them Cromwell; the Divine Right of Kings, religious intolerance that led to bloodshed, belonged to the past that everybody wanted to escape from. The last battle on English soil, the Battle of Sedgemoor, had been fought in 1685. Locke wrote his *Essay Concerning Human Understanding* in 1690.

Locke came the third Earl of Shaftesbury (1671–1713), for
ven more popular, further removed from Hobbes, more
ic, genial and readable. Hobbes in his *Leviathan* (1651)
had described the life of man as 'solitary, poor, nasty, brutish,
and short'. Shaftesbury believed that we could cure social abuses
by laughing at them. Between the pessimism of Hobbes and
Shaftesbury's facile optimism there is a wide gulf, the gulf
between the blood-drenched bitterness of the 17th century and
the 'polish and politeness' of the 18th. And Shaftesbury was
explained to the new reading public by Addison; it was the aim
of Steele and Addison, the first English journalists, to 'bring
philosophy to the coffee-houses'.

To summarise the thought of the age in a few words, you
might say it was a time when the goodness of human nature was
generally believed in. This was a reaction from Hobbes, and it
wasn't shared by Swift. Against the new, optimistic belief in the
prevalence of 'good nature' was the much older Christian belief
that man is corrupted by the sin of Adam, and lost without
Grace. This was the real conflict, which we see in the novels of
Fielding; a struggle between an optimistic and a pessimistic view
of human nature.

PELAGIUS *v.* ST. AUGUSTINE

It is convenient to represent the conflict by using these two names
as signposts. Pelagius, the Latin name of Morgan, a 4th-century
monk, believed in the heresy that the human will was capable of
good without divine Grace. In the 18th century the Pelagian
attitude represented a change of real meaning. Perhaps it is one
of the greatest changes in human thought that has occurred since
the advent of Christianity, and we see it in the works of Fielding.
The Pelagian belief is that man can save himself without the intervention of God. In society, this belief showed in an attitude of
mind; 'God,' as it has been put, 'was expelled from society'. God
was in his Heaven, but on earth we could do something about
human institutions; this was the beginning of the modern
humanitarian concern about poverty and cruelty.

St. Augustine of Hippo (d. 430), author of the *Confessions*, represents the orthodox Christian belief that the world is a vale of tears, that man is irremediably corrupted by the sin of Adam; that one's only hope lies in what Parson Adams called disapprovingly in *Joseph Andrews* 'preaching and praying', and in the next world.

Thomas Hobbes (1588–1679), though probably an atheist, was no Pelagian. Nor was Swift, with his vision of man as hideous Yahoos in his *Gulliver's Travels* (1726). Hobbes belonged to the century of bloodshed, Swift's despair was not typical of his age. More typical were the fashionable, we could say Pelagian, philosophers, Locke and Shaftesbury, and Shaftesbury's philosophy as expressed in Pope's *Essay on Man*:

One truth is clear, WHATEVER IS, IS RIGHT.

At the other extreme from this was the pessimism of Swift: '. . . last week I saw a woman flay'd, and you will hardly believe how it altered her position for the worse', he wrote in *A Tale of a Tub*.

Fielding was a pragmatist; he wanted to alter human institutions and in fact did; more than any other writer of this time he attacked the hypocrisy of those who prayed but did nothing. In all this he was Pelagian, and so were the best Christians, and the best orthodox clerics, of his time. It could be argued that there has always been something distinctively Pelagian about the Church of England, as opposed to the Augustinian orthodoxy of the Continent. Fielding was one of the new Englishmen; faced with a problem, whether scientific or social, he believed in action.

Yet, as we shall see, he believed in the intervention of Providence in human affairs. As he grew older he believed this increasingly; as a magistrate he used to hand out to those who came before him at the dock a little tract he had written on the subject: 'Examples of the Interposition of Providence in the Detection and Punishment of Murder'. One criminal is reported to have burst into tears, thinking what might have been avoided if only he had read it earlier. Fielding's belief that we must put our faith in a benign Providence, or we shall be lost, is very important to an understanding of his novels. It gives a fatalistic quality to his work; his characters don't work out their own destinies; Providence (in actual fact, of course, Fielding) works it out for them.

In this way Fielding had a foot in both camps; these two opposing modes of thought conflicted in his mind. He never resolved the conflict—probably was unaware of it—though it should be emphasised that he himself never used either of these terms. But this conflict was partly responsible for the tension in his work and for its limitations.

LOCKE, SHAFTESBURY

It is the second of these two philosophers, the less important of the two though the more fashionable at the time, who influenced Fielding widely and directly. *Tom Jones* has been described as an attempt to express Shaftesbury's doctrine in fictional form, and, in the new discovery of Fielding by the Americans, the philosophical content of his work plays a very important part. It is really the Americans who began to use the terms Pelagian and Augustinian, with reference to Fielding.

But John Locke's influence on the whole century was pervasive and immense. He was a cautious optimist. 'The truth,' he said, 'is hard to ascertain . . . a rational man will tend to doubt.' He believed in common sense and the importance of judgement in controlling what were called the 'passions'. He believed in religious freedom: 'no man should conform his faith to the dictates of another'; and in property: 'civil society, the chief end of which is civil property'. His insistence on the rights of property was particularly a feature of the age, a reaction from the interference of James II in the estates of the squires and the internal administration of the country generally, which had led to the 1688 revolution.

Shaftesbury's *Characteristics of Men, Manners, Opinions, Times* (1711) ran into many editions in the first half of the century, then was rapidly forgotten. Shaftesbury was not a systematic philosopher and was less impressed than Hobbes and Locke by the power of reason; he believed that we have a 'moral sense' that 'apprehends the rightness or wrongness of actions without recourse to reasoning'. Compare this with Hobbes's belief that reason is the servant of the desires. When Fielding's characters argue—Lady Booby (from *Joseph Andrews*) or Black George (from *Tom Jones*) arguing with themselves to try to persuade themselves that what they want is right and practicable, or Square (from *Tom Jones*) caught with Molly Seagrim by Tom himself, defending his conduct on high philosophical grounds—Fielding is illustrating Hobbes's cynical doctrine. There is no altruism in Hobbes, and there is little in Fielding. The worldliness that many critics find irritating in Fielding, the persistent cynicism, the refusal to admit that people ever do act uncalculatingly, without motive—this is a legacy of Hobbes. It helps to give a 'contrived' quality to his novels, make his characters seem like puppets, and gives the apparent smugness, 'you-and-I,-reader,-know-what's-going-on' quality to Fielding himself, pulling the strings behind. But, in all this elaborate machinery, we notice certain characters who don't reason their way through life, and they are usually right. They are not always the good characters. Squire Western (in *Tom Jones*) goes straight to the point, in the incident (IV, 3) of Sophia's tame bird; he is the one who doesn't reason, and he gets it right. You can usually say in Fielding that when a character reasons, he is in the process of misleading himself. When a character in Fielding's novels uses his own instinctive judgement, he never goes wrong. Really wicked characters like Blifil (from *Tom Jones*) don't seem to have any instinctive judgement; they are all guile and calculation.

But Shaftesbury was a 'deist', and here Fielding parted from him.

DEISM, LATITUDINARIANISM, ENTHUSIASM

The deists believed that evil was part of the pattern of the universe; we shall understand everything, when we understand the whole. Shaftesbury believed that human nature was basically good, that the world was basically good. Fielding never (so far as we know) wrote a tragedy; his novels all end on a note of rather forced, Shaftesburian optimism. But I don't believe Fielding shared Shaftesbury's optimism about human nature. Even in his sunniest novel, *Joseph Andrews*, there are incidents, such as that of Joseph and the stage coach, which show what Fielding really thought of human nature. There are times when he seems to incline towards Swift's bitter despair (as for example in his last novel, *Amelia*) but he struggles hard against it; you could not accuse Fielding of enjoying his despair, as you might possibly accuse Swift.

Fielding, pessimistic about individual human beings, remained optimistic about society. Here he agreed with Shaftesbury and the deists who said that self-interest would lead men towards benevolence and the general good of society. (This, I think, is a very American belief: its application today would be towards private enterprise and no government interference: let the people alone.) Laughter, Shaftesbury said, was the weapon for 'disentangling truth from folly'. God was the 'supreme Manager . . . best natur'd one in the World'. Evil, once we understood it, we would see as something like shading in drawing or discord in music. Pope described it:

All Nature is but Art, unknown to thee;
All Chance, Direction which thou canst not see;
All Discord, Harmony not understood;
All partial Evil, universal Good . . .   ESSAY ON MAN

Parson Adams, from *Joseph Andrews* (III, 11), echoes Pope's second line when he says, '. . . for as we know not future events, so neither can we tell to what purpose any accident tends, and that which at first threatens us with evil may in the end produce our good'. Though what Fielding believed one has sometimes to judge for oneself. Fielding likes to use ideas in his novels, 'circulating' them as Bernard Shaw circulates ideas through his plays. Square, the Platonist and philosopher (from *Tom Jones*), is to some extent a caricature of a deist; we might describe him as Pelagian too, in which case we could make Thwackum, the schoolmaster, an Augustinian. Fielding often has his tongue in his cheek. But we do know that he parted from the deists when it came to their rejecting the biblical 'reward of Heaven and punishment of Hell', sometimes called the 'rod and sweetmeat alternatives', Extreme deists like Tindall rejected the Book of Revelation and the supernatural element in the Bible; one is reminded of Bishop Robinson today and his booklet, *Honest to God*; rejecting what was difficult to reconcile with reason, they made their God vaguer and vaguer. Of the many churchmen in Fielding's works, we can be fairly sure that Parson Adams comes close to Fielding's views, and Adams was a devout, orthodox member of the 'latitudinarian' church of Fielding's time.

Latitudinarianism meant as the word suggests broad-minded-ness, comprehensiveness, tolerance. At its best it was a practical Christianity of good works and active charity. This was the Christianity of the great, orthodox bishops of the time, Tillotson and Hoadly. Reacting away from what they called 'enthusiasm', they achieved a religion in which there was little mystery, an absence of emotion and a minimum of doctrine. This is the world of Fielding's novels which are full of churchmen; the world of 'the light of day', without mystery or spirituality. Latitudinarian-ism contained only too obviously its own seeds of decay; it tended to make the clergy, as Locke saw them, a sort of police. And it opened the way to corruption, what Gibbon was to call later in the century the 'fat slumbers' of the clergy; those clergy-men like Parson Trulliber (from *Joseph Andrews*) whose Christian-ity was confined to perfunctory church services on Sunday.

When Fielding left the theatre and turned to novel-writing in the 1740s he seems to have been asking himself: what is the duty of a clergyman, what sort of person is an ideal clergyman? Parson Adams was his answer, one of the great characters in English fiction and (in my opinion) Fielding's most successful creation, who shows the latitudinarian church at its best; like Fielding the magistrate, Adams went out into the highways and byways, seeking to apply Christianity.

'Enthusiasm' was associated with Methodism and the Wesley-ans. It had a connotation in those days similar to that of 'fanatic-ism' today; suggesting not only the Wesleyan reaction to the unspiritual, worldly latitudinarian church but also all those evils associated with the Jacobites, the Stuarts who wanted to re-impose (it was popularly believed) a fanatical Catholicism. In this way it suggested both the past, the bad old days of religious strife, and the dangerous future of the Wesleys and Whitefield. An enthusiast is (literally) one with 'God inside him'; Locke defined it as 'a belief in personal revelation'. 'Enthusiasm,' Locke said, 'laying by reason, would set up revelation without it; whereby in effect it takes away both reason and revelation, and substitutes in the room of it the ungrounded fantasies of a man's own brain.' In this quotation one can see not only the 18th-century dislike of enthusiasm, but their dislike of 'fantasy'—the undisciplined world of the imagination. Locke played down the *imagination*, believed rather in the *understanding*, and the dissociation, in Fielding's day, between the imagination and the understanding was like C. P. Snow's 'two cultures' today. As Basil Williams points out (in *The Oxford History of England*, Vol. XI) nobody, in this age of satire, could have written lines like Shelley's:

> I met Murder on the way—
> He had a mask like Castlereagh— . . .

In Fielding's time one could not write like this, either in prose or verse; it was the penalty paid for the 'Age of Reason'.

THE WESLEYS AND WHITEFIELD

John Wesley (1713–91), his brother Charles, and George Whitefield, were the founders of Methodism. Wesley attacked the worldliness of the latitudinarian divines, what Fielding called the 'luxury and splendour of the clergy'. But Fielding, not very rationally, hated the Methodists. He could never resist indulging this dislike; Blifil (from *Tom Jones*), when we last hear of him, has 'turned Methodist'. It was Whitefield's form of Methodism which irritated Fielding. Whitefield broke away from the Wesleys; he believed in predestined salvation, that is, in an 'elect' who were predestined to be saved. This was a fatalistic doctrine with an implication in it that you could do what you liked if you were one of these elect. Fielding did not bother to understand Methodism very clearly but he saw Whitefield as bringing 'nonsense and enthusiasm to his aid . . . a detestable doctrine of *faith against good works* [my italics] . . . coined in hell' (*Joseph*

Andrews, I, 17). Whitefield, in Fielding's view, invited sanctimonious hypocrisy because he exalted what one said and thought over what one did. Like Mr. Peter Pounce (*Joseph Andrews*, III, 13), Whitefield seemed to prefer (though of course in fact he didn't) a 'disposition to charity'.

To sum up, 'good works' was at the centre of Fielding's religion. His characters argue, produce versions of the current philosophies, and reveal themselves; always what matters is the contrast, as it often is, between what they think in a purely abstract way and what they do. It was by the latter that Fielding judged them.

3
Early Life

Fielding was born in 1707 at Sharpham Park, Somerset. His father, Sir Edmund Fielding, a colonel and later a general, was descended from the Earls of Denbigh, and served under Marlborough. Colonel Fielding was an aristocrat. We get the impression of a high-spirited, unscrupulous, feckless man, to be glimpsed at from time to time in Fielding's work and particularly in the last novel, *Amelia* (1751).

After the signing of the Treaty of Utrecht in 1713 which ended the War of the Spanish Succession there followed a long period free of major wars, in which England, after the glories of Marlborough, settled down to the business of making money. In Colonel Fielding we probably see one of the many army officers —they are to be found in his son's last novel—who drifted about the city of London, or into the country, generally at a loss what to do and short of money; from 1712 he was on half-pay. His ancestry was a wild one though with some sober stock in it. There was a Canon of Salisbury and two brothers Fielding mentioned by Pepys, one of whom murdered the other in a drunken brawl near the 'Three Tuns Tavern'.

In 1706 Colonel Fielding married Sarah Gould, daughter of Sir Henry Gould. The Goulds were very sober; Sir Henry was a Judge of the King's Bench. It was a 'runaway match'; so was Henry Fielding's marriage, and almost every marriage in his novels. Into Fielding's ancestry come two strands, the rake and the sober judge, and the two battle with one another; and in Fielding's early boyhood, the time when according to Freud one is influenced for life, the battle was at its height. Sir Henry Gould made a will bequeathing money for a small estate to Sarah and her children but carefully excluding from the will Colonel Fielding. Sir Henry died in 1710 when Fielding was three. In that year the family had settled on the estate which was in East Stour, Dorset. Colonel Fielding went to Ireland. Then in 1718 Sarah died and the Colonel, contrary to the agreement, returned from Ireland to take over the estate.

What followed was material for the novels. According to Freud the device of 'concealed parentage' indicates 'a child's dissatisfaction with his parents', and this device Fielding employs in *Joseph Andrews* and *Tom Jones* and, incidentally, bequeathed it to the English novel. Walter Allen in *The English Novel* writes: 'It is, too, a matter of common observation that even the greatest (novelists) seem to be exploring similar types and situations from novel to novel, exploring more deeply, doubtless, in each successive book, almost as though the exploration was the result of an obsession.' Parentage and identity were to be the themes of two of Fielding's novels.

Father and grandmother (Lady Gould, widow of Sir Henry) struggled for possession of the estate. There was a succession of acrimonious law suits. Lady Gould took a house in Salisbury so that she could be near the children. In 1721 Colonel Fielding tried unsuccessfully to kidnap two of his children from their school in Salisbury. In the same year Henry, at Eton, ran away from school to his grandmother's house in Salisbury; possibly for a lark, or possibly because he feared his father was going to take him away. In an affidavit of Lady Gould's we read: '. . . children treated in a most barbarous, cruel and inhumane manner . . . fed on food of poorest quality, denied Protestant instruction, beaten . . .' This was after Colonel Fielding had weakened his case by marrying again, a widow called Anna Rapha, or Raza, who 'kept an eating House' in London. The contest was won eventually by Lady Gould.

If you think of this when you read the early, so vivid chapters of *Tom Jones* you may feel it explains a certain quality in them: it is an unreal quality, because of the isolation of Tom. There is a curious lack of intimacy between him and his guardian; he exists in a vacuum, in which misunderstandings can be disastrous. Joseph Andrews has lost his father; when he finds him, he turns out to have a tormented, guilt-ridden past. Fielding was pulled both ways—to his father, whom in many ways he resembled, on one side, and on the other side to his grandmother and her relatives, such as Davidge Gould, Fielding's uncle who was to become a 'Master of the Bench'. He ran wild, left to his own devices. In 1725, assisted by his 'man', he tried to kidnap an eighteen-year-old girl, Sarah Andrew, of Lyme Regis. There were charges of assault and counter-assault and the father of one of the girl's suitors complained that he went in fear of 'bodily hurt' from Henry Fielding. The girl was a cousin of Fielding's on the Gould side.

We get glimpses of all this from his early biographer, Arthur Murphy (the only one of Fielding's succession of biographers who knew him personally), who was deeply shocked. Very likely Fielding yearned for the friendship and esteem of his mother's family, to whom in early youth he had been closest, and lost it by his behaviour. The following passage from 'Mr. Wilson's Story' (Mr. Wilson who turned out to be the father of Joseph Andrews) is very probably autobiographical:

> ... being a forward youth, I was extremely impatient to be in the world: for which I thought my parts, knowledge, and manhood thoroughly qualified me. And to this early introduction into life, without a guide, I impute all my future misfortunes; for, besides the obvious mischiefs which attend this, there is one which hath not been so generally observed: the first impression which mankind receives of you will be very difficult to eradicate.   III, 3

The 'father-figures' of Fielding's novels, Mr. Allworthy (from *Tom Jones*), Doctor Harrison (from *Amelia*), suggest the sober outlines of the Goulds. They represent the sort of father he would have liked to have had. In the two major novels, the one, *Joseph Andrews*, very much like a trial run for the other, *Tom Jones*, we get the central theme of a rootless young man in search of the security and stability of parents.

Fielding's real father in due course became a lieutenant-general and died in 1742. Father and son seem to have maintained a

friendly relationship. In 1716 Colonel Fielding h?
while playing faro at a coffee-house in London, ?
story that Fielding made no reference in his plays t
Acts of Charles II and Anne because his father too!
the Acts to repudiate this debt dishonourably, maybe line
tain Booth (from *Amelia*) stumbling into a gambling debt which
he subsequently hopes, vaguely, he will be able to get out of
paying. Fielding was supposed to have had an allowance of £200
from his father but 'anybody might pay that would' when it
came to collecting the money.

This was no tragic, Dickensian boyhood. According to Murphy, Fielding was a very high-spirited youth, strikingly handsome, over six foot, attractive to women—in other words,
exactly like Tom Jones. And at Eton he acquired a love of
learning; Homer, Aeschylus, Aristotle, Cicero's *De Consolatione*.
These are the three elements in Fielding's make-up; the rake—
writer of 'shocking' plays and man-about-town; the moralist;
the classical scholar. It makes an odd mixture and it is not
surprising that contemporaries refused to see the second and third
elements because of the first. But in the early days when the rake
was in the ascendant there was evidence of the moralist, the
magistrate-to-be. The plays which he wrote in his twenties
were often fiercely moralistic in tone, developing the familiar,
later themes: hatred of corruption, arrogance and hypocrisy.
While following his father, whom he had probably joined in
London in 1728, he was looking back with regret to the other
side, the Goulds.

Another thing that has been suggested is that from his boyhood
comes his odd concern with the theme of incest. This motif
crops up in the two major novels, jarring the reader as a theme
that seems to belong to a different kind of novel. Colonel Fielding
was to marry three, maybe four times; he had a family by his
second wife who died in 1727. In this mixed entourage of half-
sisters and step-mothers there existed the same possibility that
Joseph Andrews faced, that his Fanny was his sister; and the risk
of Tom Jones's dilemma on finding he had made love with his
(apparent) mother. Fielding's upbringing was a strange one. The

eresting thing about it is that in various guises it winds its way down the course of the English novel, through Dickens and Thackeray, what Allen calls 'the whole outfit of missing heirs, mistaken identities, stolen children, forged wills and the rest'.

The outfit we owe to the theatre, the obsession probably comes from early experience. And from his boyhood comes that unmistakable Fielding countryside, which was East Stour, Dorset, and its neighbourhood. It was a countryside in which one encountered adventures at every turn of the road or rise of the hill, described by V. S. Pritchett as a 'mixture of gymnasium and an open-air extension of the Established Church'. Those sections of the novels that are set in the country are the sunniest, happiest ones. When he gets his characters to London a darkness settles on Fielding's work.

FIELDING'S LONDON

When Fielding came to London in 1728 George II was on the throne. In 1715, the year after George I had been brought over from Hanover, the first Jacobite rebellion had occurred. It had failed and George, who couldn't speak a word of English, was secure, and Sir Robert Walpole became his chief minister.

Walpole was Prime Minister from 1721 until 1742 without interruption and during this time Fielding became a well-known figure in London life. He spent a year from 1728 to 1729 at the University of Leyden in Holland; otherwise, till he married, he lived in London. Politically, it was marked by unsatisfactory, intermittent wars with Spain in 1727 and 1739 ('The War of Jenkins' Ear'), a threat of further Jacobite invasion which seemed to recede as the years went by but was always there and, at home, by the materialistic, corrupt, though from a practical point of view successful, policies of Walpole.

The two political parties, the names themselves originating from terms of abuse in the religious struggles of the previous century, were the Whigs and the Tories. The Tories represented the aristocracy, the church and the more powerful sections of the community, but they had let themselves become associated, particularly through their leader Bolingbroke, with the Stuart

Pretenders. The result was political complexity and confusion in which the Whigs took power. Squire Western (from *Tom Jones*) drank to the 'King over the Water' and was an orthodox Tory Jacobite, with a hatred of what he called 'Hanover rats'—it was the Whigs who had introduced the dynasty of the Georges. But he also hated the titled aristocracy, and he valued his freedom which the Catholic Stuarts would presumably have taken away from him. Out of this complexity came the good-humoured political tolerance that we see in Fielding. We take it for granted now, after two centuries, recognising in his mock election scenes in the plays the precursors of Dickens's 'Eatanswill' election (from *Pickwick Papers*). But this was new. Walpole flourished and believed that 'every man had his price'. He was attacked by the writers, the 'wits'. Almost alone on his side among these was Colley Cibber, the Poet Laureate, playwright and theatre manager, who was a figure of fun to the literary world, ridiculed by Pope in *The Dunciad* and by Fielding in his plays.

The divisions in society were never greater than at this time, and the real criterion was money. A further division that was becoming felt, and which was made much of by the later 18th-century dramatists, Goldsmith and Sheridan, was the division of town and country. The town, London, presented appalling contrasts. Irwin Ehrenpreis, in his study of *Tom Jones*, says that in Fielding's novels 'Richardson's city of shopkeepers and parish churches, of early risings and quiet routines, gets few glances'. The London of Fielding was the London of the aristocracy, the 'bohemian' literary society, and the poor.

It was the time when London was beginning to acquire those dark, sombre aspects which were to make it the 'dissolute city' of Wordsworth and the symbol of evil in Dickens's novels. Gangs roamed the main thoroughfares, one could be robbed in broad daylight in the centre of Piccadilly. Or else one was 'press-ganged'. Jonathan Wild, hanged in 1725, had organised the gangs against a background of corruption, in which the magistrate's office was widely recognised as being a way of making money. Sir Thomas Veil, Fielding's predecessor as Bow Street Magistrate, kept a private room for 'examining' attractive female defendants; the only forces of law were the watchmen: 'poor old decrepit people who are from their want of bodily strength, rendered incapable of getting a livelihood by work', as Fielding describes them in *Amelia* (I, 2); and there were the constables, citizens who were compulsorily enrolled for duty for periods of one year, on a spare-time basis. This was the time of cheap gin. By 1733 there were six thousand to seven thousand dram shops in London. An anonymous pamphlet which Fielding used when he was a magistrate contains the following description:

> In one place not far from East Smithfield, a trader has a large empty room backward, where, as his wretched guests get intoxicated, there are laid together in heaps promiscuously, men, women and children, till they recover themselves, when they proceed to drink on . . .

In Hogarth's 'Gin Lane' we can read, inscribed on the cellar door near the bottom of the picture:

> Drunk for a penny
> Dead drunk for two pennies
> Clean straw for nothing

In 1716 there were sixty thousand debtors imprisoned in England and Wales.

In contrast to this was the splendour, elegance and 'polish' of the rich. Fielding refers in *Tom Jones* (XIV, 1) to 'those strange monsters in lace and embroidery' described by writers who did not know the 'upper life' at first hand, as he did. One of the most vivid descriptions of this upper life is to be found in 'Mr. Wilson's Story':

> In the morning I arose, took my great stick, and walked out in my green frock, with my hair in papers (a groan from Adams), and sauntered about till ten. Went to the auction; told Lady—— she had a dirty face; laughed heartily at something Captain—— said, I can't remember what, for I did not very well hear it; whispered Lord——; bowed to the Duke of——; and was going to bid for a snuff-box, but did not, for fear I should have had it.
>
> JOSEPH ANDREWS III, 3

The leisured society had nothing to do except play cards or go to the assemblies at Vauxhall Gardens or, if they were inclined, the men could go to the coffee-houses and talk; in the evenings more talk, intrigue, or a visit to the 'play'.

THE PERIOD OF THE PLAYS: 1728–37

In 1728 Fielding, a young man of twenty-one loose in London, decided to write plays; inspired, maybe, by the tremendous success of *The Beggar's Opera*. He wrote in all about twenty-eight, of which only one is widely known today. You may find an abridged version of *The Tragedy of Tragedies; or the Life and Death of Tom Thumb the Great*, which he wrote in 1730, in a collection of humorous plays for children. It is worth reading in a full version, with Fielding's 'annotations', written under his pseudonym of 'Scriblerus Secundus' (Pope and Swift and their friends had collectively been the first Scriblerus). Taking the idea from a 'chap-book' ballad, 'In Arthur's Court Tom Thumb did live', Fielding parodies the inflated diction, 'rhodomontade', of Dryden, Thomson, Lee, Philips and other Restoration dramatists —there are forty-two identified hits at these in the text. For example, Thomson's lines from *New Sophonisba:*

Oh! Sophonisba, Sophonisba, oh!
Oh! Narva, Narva, oh!

become:

Grizzle: Oh! Huncamunca, Huncamunca, oh!
Thy pouting breasts, like kettle-drums of brass,
Beat everlasting loud alarms of joy . . .   2, 5

and the play ends, Shakespeare-like, in total massacre of the characters.

Lady Mary Wortley Montagu, the traveller and letter-writer, who was Fielding's cousin, encouraged him to write his first play, *Love in Several Masques*, and sat through the three or four performances it received. It was the same year (1728) when *The Beggar's Opera* 'made Gay rich and Rich gay', Rich being the theatre manager. Gay's masterpiece was a new idea and Fielding used it as he tried most of the dramatic forms except tragedy, but not with the same success; maybe because Gay, writing the first 'ballad opera', had taken the best tunes. It was an experimental period. Pantomime and Italian opera were introduced to England at this time. In plays such as *The Author's Farce* (1730), Fielding derided the 'foreign' music of Handel. In this he shared the view of Squire Western, from the later *Tom Jones*, and he wrote two songs at this time of the sort Squire Western was to like; *When mighty roast beef was the Englishman's food* and *The dusky night rides down the sky*, from *Don Quixote in England* (1734). Later, when his Little Theatre had been closed by Act of Parliament and a company of French players tried to perform in it, the audience drowned the performance by singing the former of these songs.

When Joseph Andrews went to London (I, 4) 'he led the opinion of all the other footmen at an opera' and 'was a little too forward in riots, at the playhouses and assemblies'. If plays are determined by audience, the audience then was rowdy, not very critical. 'The town, like a peevish child, knows not what it desires, and is always best pleased with a rattle', the poet says to the player in *Joseph Andrews* (III, 10). The actors and actresses were more important than the plays. Fielding was not making a literary reputation. Later, when he tried his hand at law, it probably prevented him from getting any briefs. He was becoming notorious; the footmen and others who yelled out his songs in 1738 in the face of the French company had, on an earlier occasion, hissed his play off the stage after a single performance.

Restoration Comedy—the term comes from the return of the theatre with the restoration of the monarchy in 1660—'the comedy of manners', as it has been called, was based on the idea of the 'wit' who takes everything lightly, never loses his head or his heart and regards morality as absurdly 'middle-class'. It was the way of life picked up by the exiled English cavaliers at the court of Louis XIV. It had worked itself out through Wycherley (1640–1716), Congreve (1670–1729), and Vanbrugh, who had died in 1726, his last play, *The Provok'd Wife*, being put on after his death by Colley Cibber in 1728. These plays were at their best very thin and heartless. The tradition of sophisticated mockery, of hostility to Puritanism which now became hostility to all serious, moral ideas, lingered on. But there was a strain something new, a desire to achieve something more solid vacuum left after the death of Vanbrugh. If you go British Museum or a similar institution and look throug collections of plays that followed Vanbrugh's death you will find, among Fielding's comedies and burlesques, more solemn imitations of Shakespeare like the following, from an anonymous play entitled *King Charles I*:

> Cromwell· Now, thro' the maze of gloomy policy,
> Has fire-ey'd Faction work'd her way to light,
> And deck'd Ambition in the robe of Power . . .

No wonder Fielding felt the urge to parody. The most successful 'serious' play of the century had been Addison's *Cato*, which seems lifeless, dry and academic today.

Fielding was learning how to write, and he was deciding with Vanbrugh that 'the business of comedy is to show people what they should do, by representing them on the stage doing what they should not'. His plays all give the impression of having been dashed off in a hurry. According to Murphy, he wrote on 'tobacco-paper'. In a period of five years he wrote seventeen of them. He attacked Colley Cibber, and his son Theophilus, for the way they tampered with Shakespeare: 'My father and I, sir, are a couple of poetical tailors; when a play is brought us, we consider it as a tailor doth his coat, we cut it, sir, we cut it.' One of the most amusing and better constructed plays, well worth a revival, I think, is *The Old Debauchees*. This was based on the scandal at Toulon in which a Jesuit priest was supposed to have seduced a nun, using sorcery. Strongly anti-Catholic in tone, it offended Pope. In this play is Jourdain, J.P., one of the first of Fielding's Justices: 'I never punish any vice but property'; and there is a character, Old Caroon, who has the exuberance of Western: 'Well, I never made a hole in a gown yet, I never have tapped a priest: but if I don't let out some reverend blood before the sun sets, may I never see him rise again. I'll carbonade the villain, I'll make a Ragout for the Devil's Supper of him.'

We get pictures of the life he lived; impecunious scribblers facing nagging landladies and dunning creditors, and he attacked 'high life' with heavy-handed ferocity. Running through all his plays, satirical or merely farcical, there was a moral undertone. He was developing a good ear for dialogue: 'But rape and murder no gentleman need be ashamed of, and this is an honest brother ravisher' (from *Rape upon Rape*, 1730). About a lot of these attacks there seems to be a gay, absent-minded quality; the ensuing opposition obviously surprised him. Fielding had neither the viciousness nor the thin skin of Pope. One or two of the plays, such as *Pasquin* (1736), became very successful. Two of the best are adaptations of Molière: *The Mock Doctor* (1732) and *The Miser* (1733).

Voltaire praised these; perhaps if he had gone on writing plays Fielding would have written something worthy of Molière. He had the classical scholarship to appreciate the tight construction of Molière's plays as opposed to the loose freedom of Shakespeare. His plays are just good enough, with their many excellent lines, I think, to be disappointing. As it was, he was to approach his novels from the theatre. To take one example here, the concealment scene from *Tom Jones* (XV, 7), when Jones hides Mrs. Honour from Lady Bellaston, who then tries to hide while Jones copes with the drunken Nightingale, and discovers Mrs. Honour, is not only obviously theatrical in itself but was very likely to model for the 'screen scene' in Sheridan's *The School for Scandal* (1777). In this way the theatre influenced the novel which influenced the theatre.

But Fielding's satire was becoming increasingly political; he was attacking Walpole. The theme was 'greatness', the irresponsible worship of power. In *The Welsh Opera* (1731), the King was a Welsh squire called Ap-Skinken, and Walpole was Robin, his factotum; in 1737 the *Daily Gazetteer* warned him he was harming the government 'at home and abroad'. Finally, as a result of successive attacks culminating in *The Historical Register for the Year 1736* (1737), and *Eurydice Hiss'd* of the same year, in which Walpole became 'Mr. Pillage', the Prime Minister in 1737 introduced a Licensing Act which revived the old Elizabethan office of 'Master of the Revels', by which all plays had to be licensed by the Lord Chamberlain under a penalty of £50. This is the Act which is still in force and opposed by the modern 'realistic' school of dramatists. It was brought in to extinguish Fielding, which it did.

Like these modern realists, Fielding was to come under fire for portraying squalor; 'low life', as it was called then. But it was the political satire that extinguished him as a playwright. In the words of Colley Cibber, who managed one of the two 'patent' theatres that were exempt from the Act, he had 'set fire to his stage, by writing up to an Act of Parliament to demolish it'. Fielding was now thirty; married and notorious. What was he to do next?

4

The Period of the Novels

MARRIAGE AND MIDDLE LIFE

'Why did he draw his Heroine so fond, so foolish, and so insipid?' Richardson wrote, referring to Sophia, from *Tom Jones*.

Fielding's heroes and heroines are physically beautiful; he dwells on their fleshly glories, at a time when he was losing his own youth and health, changing from the handsome young man who kidnapped Sarah Andrews at Lyme Regis to the grotesque, dropsical figure of the last years. He married his first wife, Charlotte Cradock, in 1734 and she was (we are told) the model for these beautiful, physically-irresistible women: Amelia, Sophia, and probably Fanny from *Joseph Andrews*, not to mention Mrs. Heartfree from *Jonathan Wild*.

It is interesting to speculate how important this was to the subsequent history of the novel. Fielding bequeathed to it these ideal portraits of femininity, seen from the man's point of view. Of the three Sophia, in my opinion, is the most subtle portrait. Sophia has her little moments of vanity. But really, these three ladies are faultless; they are women as men would like them to be and this idealised, faultless woman became a weakness, a great potential source of sentimentality, in the English novel. The French (think of Laclos, Stendhal, Flaubert) examined their womenfolk thoughtfully. But think of Thackeray's Amelia in *Vanity Fair* (the same name is itself significant); the word 'mother' alone, was enough to stultify Thackeray's critical faculty, sending him into a state of rapt adoration. Thackeray in fact imitated all Fielding's worst features. Or think of Dora, the 'child-wife' of Dickens's *David Copperfield*. Read Fielding's last novel, *Amelia*, and then read Chapters 35 ('Widow and Mother') and 38 ('A

Family in a Very Small Way') of *Vanity Fair*, and Chapters 48 and 53 of *David Copperfield* and you may agree that Fielding influenced these passages.

I don't believe that the charge of sentimentality can be levelled against Fielding, except possibly in *Amelia*—if by sentimentality we mean, as I take it to mean, emotional self-indulgence. Fielding's life was grim and guilt-ridden; he loved his wife and his 'little home', but lived like a rake; Charlotte and her children had a bleak, hard life. *Amelia* is probably a fairly faithful record of it. She died young, leaving him 'frantic with grief', and there is genuine agony, genuine deep regret and love, in Fielding's domestic scenes, in his successive, loving portraits of an ideal woman, no more sentimental than is Milton's moving sonnet 'On his deceased wife':

> . . . Love, sweetness, goodness, in her person shined
> So clear as in no face with more delight.
> But, oh! as to embrace me she inclined,
> I waked, she fled, and day brought back my night.

In contrast to this, Dickens was enjoying himself with Dora and so was Thackeray with his Amelia.

Fielding's marriage was a 'runaway match'. But shortly afterwards Charlotte's mother died and left her daughter £1,500. For the first and last time in his life Fielding had funds. Here, according to Murphy, is how they got through the money:

> To East Stour he retired with his wife on whom he doated, with a resolution to bid adieu to all the follies and intemperances to which he had addicted himself in the career of a town life. But unfortunately a kind of family pride here gained the ascendancy over him and he began immediately to vie in splendour with the neighbouring country squires. With an estate not much above two hundred pounds a year and his wife's fortune, which did not exceed fifteen hundred pounds, he encumbered himself with a large retinue of servants, all clad in costly yellow liveries. For their master's honour, these people could not descend so low as to be careful of their apparel, but in a month or two were unfit to be seen; the squire's dignity required that they should be new-equipped; and his chief pleasure consisting in society and convivial mirth, his hospitality

threw open his doors and in less than three years, entertainments, hounds and horses, entirely devoured a little patrimony.

Lady Bute, the daughter of Lady Mary Wortley Montagu, gave a picture of his married life after this:

> He loved her passionately and she returned his affection, yet had no happy life. For they were seldom in a state of quiet and safety. All the world knows what was his imprudence; if he possessed a score of pounds, nothing could keep him from lavishing it idly, or make him think of the morrow.

Murphy described Fielding's life after he had been driven from the theatre as burdened by 'severities of want and pain' and harassed by bailiffs, though contemporaries spoke also of his inner contentment. He decided to become a barrister; from this time onwards becoming less and less a rake, more and more inclining towards the Gould side of the family. The 'broken wit', as Cibber described him, 'great tatter'd bard', as he rather self-consciously described himself, joined the Inner Temple to study Law and qualified as a barrister in the unusually short time of three years. His cousin, Henry Gould, had been called to the Bar in 1734. With the law he found his true vocation, though he had to wait fifteen years for success in it. Gradually, the lawyer and the moralist gained the ascendant in him. The two major novels belong to the period between 1742 and 1749 when he still had his zest for life, tolerance and humour. But he had lost the recklessness, the devil-may-care attitude; he worked at the law, and he later worked at his novels, particularly *Tom Jones*, as he had never worked at his plays.

Of this zest for life, Lady Montagu gave a description:

> His happy constitution (even when he had, with great pains, half demolished it) made him forget everything when he was before a venison pasty, or over a flask of champaigne, and I am persuaded he has known more happy moments than any prince upon the earth.

Something of Booth (from *Amelia*) is in Fielding, who Lady Montagu said was a close self-portrait. Like Booth he never held on to money. 'Friendship has called for the money,' he is reported to have said, 'the tax-collector must call again.' For his appearance at this time we can go to *Amelia* (XI, 1):

'He handsome!' cries James. 'What, with a nose like the proboscis of an elephant, with the shoulders of a porter, and the legs of a chairman? The fellow hath not in the least the look of a gentleman; and one would rather think he hath followed a plough than a camp all his life.'

This again is Fielding talking about himself, but the portrait by Hogarth (see cover) reinforces this impression of a big bluff man with a humorous mouth and a projecting chin. David Garrick and Hogarth became his friends in theatre days. Hogarth, with his strong moral feeling, his compassion and his absolutely unrelenting realism, was one of the influences which changed Fielding from the rather shallow playwright to the major novelist. Look at the faces in any Hogarth print and you see individuals, not types or species. Three times in *Tom Jones* Fielding refers his reader to Hogarth to illustrate a scene or a character; and in the preface to *Joseph Andrews* he points out that the faces in Hogarth are never distorted from the truth—unlike most literary 'burlesque'.

He was called to the Bar in 1740. Murphy speaks of his 'intense application'. The previous year he had entered a new field, that of political journalism. He wrote for and partly owned *The Champion Journal*, using the name of 'The Celebrated Captain Hercules Vinegar Bottle . . . Champion of Virtue, Honour and Freedom'. From this time till his death in 1754 his life became steadily more crowded, but for the moment there was a blank period. He roamed the Western Circuit, but as a barrister he was a total failure, probably because he was notorious as a 'scribbler'. He had many enemies now; he was attacked consistently in a journal called *Old England*. In 1743 many lawyers of the time were ridiculed in an anonymous satire called 'Causidicade', which was falsely ascribed to Fielding. Pope, Richardson, Smollett, Horace Walpole (son of the Prime Minister), Johnson—the list of those who disliked or despised him is an impressive one. In his 'farewell to the reader' from *Tom Jones*, he defends himself:

No man detests and despises scurrility more than myself; nor hath any man more reason; for none has ever been treated with more; and what is a very severe fate, I have had some of the abusive

writings of those very men fathered upon me, who, in other of their
works, have abused me themselves with the utmost virulence.

XVIII, 1

The attacks gained in virulence as Fielding became famous as a
novelist and then as a magistrate. The contrast between the
novelist, apparently indulging in squalor for the sake of squalor,
and the magistrate who should be correcting those very sins, was
one that particularly amused his enemies. What is true is that—
just as the rake had always had a strain in him of the moralist—so
the later magistrate still showed gleams of the old Fielding.
Horace Walpole had an anecdote of friends finding him 'banquet-
ing with a blind man, three Irishmen, and a whore' at his house
in Bow Street—though the 'whore' was probably his second wife.
From the days of his friendship with Hogarth he was one of those,
a small group that included men like Captain Coram, founder
of the Foundling Hospital (1745), who looked below the polish
and politeness to the squalor beneath. As he grew older the
squalor of life began to obsess him.

THE PERIOD OF THE MAJOR NOVELS: 1742–9

In 1740 Samuel Richardson, a middle-aged bookseller, published
a novel called *Pamela, or Virtue Rewarded.* It would be impossible
to conceive in fiction two more direct opposites than Fielding
and Richardson. Richardson's school name was 'serious and
gravity'; at the age of ten he wrote an anonymous letter to a
widow rebuking her for malicious gossip, and at thirteen was
'ghost-writing' the love-letters of girls in his neighbourhood.
Out of this grew, in 1739, a commission to compose a volume of
Familiar Letters as a guide for young girls going out into the
world, and out of this grew *Pamela.*

Pamela is a story of a young servant girl who stands siege
from a lecherous squire and holds out, against impossible odds,
till at the end of Volume I he marries her. In Volume II as the
squire's lady she establishes herself in society, winning over all
opposition by the sheer naked power of her 'goodness'. The
story is told in the form of letters, mostly the letters of Pamela,
whose 'conspicuous literacy' is matched only by her goodness

and her chastity; 'Like the snow, that lay last week, upon the earth and all her products,' a contemporary wrote, '(Pamela) covers every other image, with her own unbounded whiteness.' It was aimed at the new middle class and at every servant girl who dreamt of bettering herself; at Slough the village blacksmith read it out and when at last 'Squire B.' married Pamela his audience ran out and rang the church bells. Pope said the book 'will do more good than many volumes of sermons'.

The novel was a tremendous success. But Fielding saw at once that there was something not only unpleasant but false at the centre of it. The moral of it was, as he saw it, 'if the Master is not a fool, they will be debauched by him; if he is a fool, they will marry him'. Among those who raved over *Pamela* was Colley Cibber, and in 1741 an anonymous parody appeared, 'Shamela . . . by Conny Keyber', which turned *Pamela* inside out. Pamela becomes, what she was, a fortune-hunter, using her 'virtue' to trap the squire: 'I thought once of making a little fortune by my person. I now intend to make a great one by my virtue', she writes to her mother.

Literary-detective work done by Americans has shown recently without doubt that *Shamela*—as was always suspected—was written by Fielding. Then the following year he wrote *Joseph Andrews*. Joseph is the brother of Pamela, whose surname had been Andrews and who makes a brief appearance in Fielding's novel, this time under her own name. But *Joseph Andrews* takes off on its own with a new character, Parson Adams, who has no counterpart in Richardson, though he has something in him of Cervantes's *Don Quixote*, who was the subject of one of Fielding's plays. Whether *Joseph Andrews* started off as another *Shamela* and then changed course, or whether Fielding from the beginning had this second character in mind, and whether Richardson and Cervantes fuse together (along with Fielding's 'epic' theory of the novel) is matter for argument. *Joseph Andrews*, the first important 'modern' novel, has a most complicated ancestry, and a preface which reads today like something very remote and academic. But the text, after this, comes as a surprise; sunny, genial, with a great, delightful character in it,

Parson Adams, who in my opinion is Fielding's greatest creation.

In 1741 his father died. The following year he lost a favourite daughter. According to Murphy he was desperate for money. *Joseph Andrews* crept slowly into public favour; the poet Gray gave it faint praise. Fielding tried writing plays again, which failed; he wrote 'The full Vindication of the Duchess of Marlborough', which she ignored. Walpole fell from power in 1742 and possibly Fielding expected to receive patronage from the Opposition (as those Whigs who had rebelled against Walpole were called). If so, he was disappointed. To imagine the quality of his life at this time you should probably read *Amelia*. He was trying many different things, translating Aristophanes and attempting, without success, to make a living as a barrister.

In 1742 he advertised his *Miscellanies*. He had made friends with Ralph Allen of Bath who became his patron and was a model for Mr. Allworthy in *Tom Jones*. With the assistance of men like Allen £700 was raised in private subscription for the *Miscellanies*, which were published in 1743 in three volumes. The Prince of Wales headed the list of subscribers, which included most of the literary men of the day with the conspicuous exceptions of Pope and Johnson. In the third volume was a prose satire, *Jonathan Wild the Great*, based on the story of the master criminal who had been hanged in 1725. The intention was to make this into a satire on 'greatness' in general, including Walpole's, putting Newgate Gaol with the 'palaces of the great'. It was widely praised (for example by Coleridge) up to about fifty years ago; to the modern reader I think the attempt to equate Walpole with Wild, the highwayman, doesn't quite come off.

Then in 1744 Mrs. Fielding died, two years after he had lost his daughter. It was the great tragedy of his life. After this, though not at once, his writings lost their gaiety. Here, in *Amelia*, is his married life:

> To bed then she went, but not to sleep. Thrice indeed she told the dismal clock, and as often heard the more dismal watchman, till her miserable husband found his way home, and stole silently like a thief to bed to her; at which time, pretending then first to awake, she threw her snowy arms around him; though, perhaps, the more

Fielding had often behaved like Captain Booth, and this accentuated his grief. After this there is an increasing struggle in his work between optimism and pessimism, and I think after *Tom Jones* it becomes guilt-ridden. George Saintsbury referred to the 'immense pessimism' of *Jonathan Wild*. Fielding had described 'good nature' in his *Champion* journal, which had ceased publication in 1741: 'this makes us gentle without fear, humble without hopes, and charitable without ostentation'. 'Good nature'—how prevalent it is and what it means—is the theme that runs through his writings now. In his thinking he was orthodox, not powerful or original, but this struggle to remain optimistic, to retain his faith in the ultimate triumph of 'good nature', gives an urgency to his work in these last ten years of his life.

He began to believe that one must put one's trust absolutely in Providence. This is Mrs. Heartfree's final message from *Jonathan Wild*: 'that Providence will sooner or later procure the felicity of the virtuous and innocent'. His faith in Providence may have inhibited him from developing his characters and given a contrived quality, a shallowness, to his work. But the belief itself wasn't shallow, it was a strongly-held conviction that we must put our trust in God in this world; alone, he thought (and here he moved away from Shaftesbury and the deists) we are lost; our 'good nature' is not sufficient.

His work at this period included a preface to the novel, *David Simple*, by his sister, Sarah Fielding, and a grim work of fantasy in the style later called the 'Gothic', *The Journey from this World to the Next* which, like *Jonathan Wild*, was included in the *Miscellanies*. The only work from the three volumes of *Miscellanies* which is still in print, so far as I know, is *Jonathan Wild*.

Then occurred the Second Stuart Rebellion of 1745. When the English under Cope were defeated at Preston Pans panic swept the country. Fielding threw himself into political journalism. He published a 'Serious Address to the People of Great Britain', and in November of that year started another journal, *The True*

Patriot. It is interesting to compare this rather frenzied activity with the good-humoured way in which the Rebellion is described, retrospectively, in *Tom Jones*, which he probably started to write during the next two or three years. 1745 was a year of hysteria and anti-Popish fury, followed by reaction. Culloden was fought, followed by savage reprisals against the Scots who, no longer to be afraid of, became romantic; the way was paved for Robert Burns, Walter Scott, Balmoral Castle. In 1747 this process was already under way; Fielding founded a second patriotic paper, the *Jacobite Journal*, in which he adopted the name of 'John Trott-Plaid Esq.'. Jacobitism was now a fashion and he set out to attack it 'by laughing at it', the method of attacking abuses recommended by Shaftesbury in his *Characteristics of Men, Manners, Opinions, Times*. In fact Fielding's patriotism, and a 'John Bull' quality in his work which some people dislike, was always good-humoured and reflective. He has been accused of being anti-foreign (for example his dislike of Handel) but foreigners, like the French sea-captain in *Jonathan Wild*, who alone did not force his desires on Mrs. Heartfree, can behave better in his novels than Englishmen. His laughter is always thoughtful and can be turned on himself.

In 1747 he re-married; his second wife was Charlotte's maid, 'very ugly . . .' but 'full of tenderness, faithfulness and courage'; also she was five months pregnant. This gave a fine opportunity to his enemies, which now included two papers, the *London Evening Post* and *Old England*. Smollett, in a passage later omitted from his novel, *Peregrine Pickle* (1751), was referring to this and Fielding's later appointment as magistrate when he wrote: 'When he is inclined to marry his own cook-wench his gracious patron may condescend to give the bride away; and may finally settle him in his old age as a trading Westminster Justice'. Smollett was a Scotsman, which may have accounted for his dislike of Fielding. According to one source he believed Fielding stole some of the characters in *Tom Jones* from his novel, *Roderick Random*, of 1748. He may have been jealous; Fielding for some time now had enjoyed the patronage of George Lyttelton, the Opposition politician, which apparently annoyed Smollett.

Fielding was touchy, on the defensive about his new wife; you can see that in his posthumous *Voyage to Lisbon*. Though he was beginning to make some influential friends, the standard attack on him at this time was that his work was squalid, that he described 'low life', as for example in these lines by Horace Walpole:

Fielding met his bunter Muse,
And as they quaffed the Fiery Juice,
Droll Nature stamp'd each lucky hit
With unimaginable wit.

—'bunter' being a female gatherer of street refuse.

But at last he was acquiring a reputation as a lawyer. According to some reports he published about this time 'Proposals for a new law-book', now lost. In 1748, with the help of Lyttelton, he was enrolled as a magistrate. In the previous year Richardson had published the first volumes of his *Clarissa Harlowe*. This, though like *Pamela* based on what has been called 'the principle of the procrastinated rape', is a much more considerable work. A vast novel of over a million words, and like its predecessor in the form of letters, it describes a seduction in which the principal characters, Lovelace the villain and Clarissa the heroine, destroy one another.

Among recent discoveries has been a letter of Fielding's dated October 1748 in which he writes to Richardson and praises *Clarissa*. The following year he published *Tom Jones*.

FIELDING AS MAGISTRATE: 1749–54

He took office as Bow Street Magistrate in 1749, and the rest of his life is a story of achievement. The attacks on him did not cease, but when he died five years later he had made an important contribution to English Law. He was now, after *Tom Jones*, really too busy to write. *Tom Jones*, which annoyed Doctor Johnson so much ('I am shocked to hear you quote from so vicious a book,' he said of it), had a great success, what we should call a *succès de scandale*; it was the first of the great 'shocking' books, widely condemned from the pulpit, thought to be responsible for earthquakes. It was assumed that the author of this work, which had as its hero—it was even on the title-page—a 'foundling', would be a corrupt magistrate. Tom Jones was '*l'homme moyen sensuel*'—a young man who had all the weaknesses of the average young man and gave way to them. In his introduction to the first Book Fielding describes his subject matter as 'human nature'. On this theme he weaves the most complex patterns; the novel, one of the most elaborate in design ever written, has been acclaimed for its subtlety and complexity by some, condemned by others as artificial, a vast, empty shell. At the time the main complaint was at Fielding's realism in portraying Tom Jones as he was, with such obvious gusto. This was what annoyed Johnson, who kept his own desires under tight repression. *Tom Jones* is about a young man who sins and gets away with it; that he suffers for this—that his intentions, his 'nature', were good—was not enough for Johnson.

As for the office of London magistrate, to offer it to a gentleman was regarded by some as an insult, anyway. One of these London magistrates could not spell his own name. There was a property qualification which Lyttelton secured for Fielding but the job was, as Smollett had said, a 'trading' one. Fielding said himself that the £500 he was expected to receive annually (there was no official salary) was the 'dirtiest' money on earth; by not accepting bribes he reduced it to £300. Lady Montagu said of it: 'The highest of his preferment [was] raking in the lowest sinks of vice and misery. I should think it a nobler and less nauseous employment to be one of the staff officers that conduct the nocturnal weddings.' *Old England* described him as follows:

Now in the ancient shop at Bow
(He advertises it for show).
   He signs the missive warrant,
The midnight wh—re and thief to catch
He sends the constable and watch
   Expert upon the errand.
From thence he comfortably draws
Subsistence out of every cause
   For dinner and a bottle.

The second line refers to the 'Universal Register Office' which

Fielding set up with his half-brother, John (later Sir John) Fielding. This dealt in houses, livings, pistols, snuff-boxes; an experiment in a supermarket of the time.

With his assistant, Saunders Welch, Fielding set about clearing the gangs from London. His increasing reputation is shown by the fact that in 1749 he was asked to deliver the *Charge to the Grand Jury of Westminster*, a notable legal honour. But his health was deteriorating; he was suffering from gout, asthma and dropsy. The youth who had been so good-looking, the 'Adonis' of the novels, was now a figure, as he recorded with detachment at the end of his life, whom pregnant women superstitiously avoided.

But now near the end of his life he had found his vocation, and his activity increased as his health declined. *An Enquiry into the Causes of the Late Increase of Robbers* (1751) and *Proposal for a New Poor Law* succeeded one another. Fielding's attitude to law reform was conservative like that of his mentor Locke. He was against public execution but not against capital punishment, for example; private hanging, he argued, was more 'impressive'. In the *Enquiry* he advocated restraining 'the lower order of people' from the places of amusement such as Vauxhall Gardens; the rich had a right to their leisure. In the novels Fielding was no critic of the social order. The unnamed, obscenely repulsive 'Lord' in *Amelia*, and the gamekeeper-turned-poacher, Black George, in *Tom Jones*, were judged in the light of their station in life. The idea that reform, not punishment, should be the basis of law would have struck Fielding, like most of his contemporaries, as absurd. The universal reaction to the increase in crime was to increase the punishment; by the end of George II's reign (1760) there were some one hundred and sixty capital offences, which included 'cutting down a cherry tree' and 'being seen for a month in the company of Egyptians [gypsies]'. Fielding was against the lack of proportion of offence to punishment:

> 'Jesu!' said the Squire, 'would you commit two persons to Bridewell for a twig?' 'Yes,' said the lawyer, 'and with great lenity too; for if we had called it a young tree, they would have been both hanged.'   JOSEPH ANDREWS, IV, 5

Probably the most often-quoted incident in the novels is that of the postilion in *Joseph Andrews* who gave Joseph his coat and was later 'transported for robbing a hen-roost'. Fielding's satire may have done more than his activity on the bench to create a new attitude of mind. But an extreme reluctance either to change laws or bring in new ones was one of the legacies of James II's brief, catastrophic reign.

His main single achievement was the founding of a detective force, which replaced the decrepit watchmen and the constables. This was really the beginning of the modern police force—a force of men strong enough not only to apprehend felons but to 'break up the nests and retreats of criminals'. He was involved in two celebrated law cases, defending his position both times with pamphlets. The law was replacing literature, but in 1751 he published his last novel, *Amelia*.

Amelia is a domestic novel, what we should call a 'straight' novel, and its theme is adultery. Unadorned by comic exaggeration, it is the story of the married life of an army officer, Captain Booth, who Lady Montagu said was just like her cousin. Fielding was paid £1,000 for it, it was his own favourite, but it was unenthusiastically received by critics and public. Amelia's 'broken nose' was ridiculed by Smollett, and 'puffs' of the Universal Register Office annoyed others (these are missed out of the subsequent editions). *Amelia* pleased some people who disliked the other novels; Dr. Johnson read it right through without stopping. V. S. Pritchett thinks that Dickens was more influenced by this than by the earlier Fielding. Today, I think it makes heavy reading; Fielding has lost his spark. Worse, the 'confessional' Fielding who makes short appearances in the 'episodes' of the earlier novels is here throughout; one is aware of the magistrate all the time, with a guilty conscience. The best scenes are those in which he describes his domestic life, and there are some good, brief pictures of army life. The novel really fails, if it fails, with Captain Booth who, if he was in truth like Fielding, was Fielding with his best qualities omitted. Booth is a negative, defeatist character.

In 1752 he founded his fourth and best journal, *The Covent*

Garden Journal. As 'Sir Alexander Drawcansir, Censor of Great Britain', he attacked scandal and bad books; this journal played a big part in 'reforming the brutal manners of the age' which, as he grew older, had become one of his main objectives.

A pamphlet he brought out at this time: 'Examples of the Interposition of Providence in the Detection and Punishment of Murder', priced 6d. and handed out from the bench to those who came before him and advocated for schools in *The Covent Garden Journal*, illustrates, I think, his simplicity of mind. He was never a subtle character (in the way, for example, that Richardson was) and he became simpler as he grew older. At forty-seven he gives an impression of being older than he was, a figure of weight and dignity, very touchy that respect should be paid to his second wife, and an orthodox, latitudinarian Christian. Perhaps he believed so strongly now that one should put one's trust fatalistically in Providence because the only alternative to this for him, after the deaths of his first wife and daughter, would have been despair—which Fielding, unlike Captain Booth, did not indulge in for long. One scheme followed another. In 1753 he occupied himself with Poor Law reform; his scheme for 'County Houses', each to hold 5,000 paupers, with chaplains and shops, included detailed drawings. He believed with Locke that the remedy for poverty was to make the poor work. Yet at this time, when a child of ten could be hanged for stealing, Fielding described English law as 'in so mild a manner mild and gentle'.

He began a reply to an attack on the Christian faith by the Jacobite philosopher, Bolingbroke, and he became, with a salary of £200 a year, the first 'stipendiary magistrate'. With Saunders Welch he had taken Members of Parliament on a tour of the worst districts of London: '. . . if we were to make a progress through the outskirts of the town', he had written in his *Proposal*, '. . . we should behold such pictures of human misery as must move the compassion of every heart that deserves the name of human.'

One gets the impression he was about to enter on a new life. In an effort to find health he set out on a voyage to Lisbon with his second wife. But by this time he was requiring regular medical attention. The voyage was an ordeal and, as far as its original purpose was concerned, a failure. He died in Lisbon shortly after landing there. But he kept a journal of this, which was only his second expedition abroad, which is full of his active curiosity about the life around him, with discussions in the style of Addison's *Spectator* on subjects evoked by the passing scene. One gets the impression that had he lived he might have followed this with something non-fictional, in the style of Defoe's *Tour through the Whole Island of Great Britain* of 1724. Under the title of *The Journal of a Voyage to Lisbon* it was published posthumously and not well received, presumably because Fielding, so near his end, was so full of life and lacking in repentance for his sins. It ends with his arrival in Lisbon, 'the nastiest city in the world'. In the following he describes the operation of getting him aboard ship:

> However, by the assistance of my friend Mr. Welch, whom I never think or speak of but with love and esteem, I conquered this difficulty, as I did afterwards that of ascending the ship, into which I was hoisted with more ease by a chair lifted with pulleys. . . . I think, upon my entrance into the boat, I presented a spectacle of the highest horror. The total loss of limbs was apparent to all who saw me, and my face contained marks of a most diseased state, if not of death itself. Indeed, so ghastly was my countenance, that timorous women with child had abstained from my house, for fear of the ill consequences of looking at me. In this condition I ran the gauntlope (so I think I may justly call it) through rows of sailors and water-men, few of whom failed of paying their compliments to me by all manner of insults and jests on my misery. No man who knew me will think I conceived any personal resentment at this behaviour; but it was a lively picture of that cruelty and inhumanity in the nature of man which I have often contemplated with concern, and which leads the mind into a train of very uncomfortable and melancholy thoughts.   VOYAGE TO LISBON 202

But this mood did not remain with him. Like Swift, he was aware of man's 'cruelty and inhumanity'; but he struggled against a pessimism which was merely hopeless. The last entry is a cheerful one.

5

'Joseph Andrews': 1. Sources and Structure

We can distinguish at least four important influences on Fielding's first novel.

1. There was Richardson's *Pamela*. We would expect a negative influence, inasmuch as Fielding wanted to do something as different from *Pamela* as possible. He had surely done with parody, having written *Shamela*. But Pamela obsessed him, as she obsessed everybody. In *Joseph Andrews* he keeps Pamela's surname, and Squire B., which Richardson cleverly left like this, with its hint of a real person concealed and which had become Booby in *Shamela*, links with the Boobys of *Joseph Andrews*. Lady Booby is the wife of 'an uncle of Mr. Booby by the father's side'. So the anonymous Mr. B. becomes Booby; Pamela appears under her own name, and the story begins (Chapter 2): 'Mr. Joseph Andrews, the hero of our ensuing history, was esteemed to be the only son of Gaffer and Gammer Andrews, and brother to the illustrious Pamela, whose virtue is at present so famous.' In this way the families are linked.

2. There was *Don Quixote*. This was a Spanish satirical romance, written in 1605 by Cervantes, which had appealed to Fielding since his theatre days, when he wrote the play *Don Quixote in England*. On the title page of *Joseph Andrews* Fielding wrote, 'Written in imitation of the manner of Cervantes', and a glance at the two novels will show how Fielding imitates Cervantes's chapter headings. I think this influence is very much on the surface. There is a similarity between Don Quixote, the knight who, refusing to face reality, lives in an imaginary world of chivalry, and tilts at windmills and flocks of sheep, mistaking them for giants and armies, and Parson Adams, who never sees

the meanness of the people around him till it is forced on him, and both are tall, gawky, gaunt and ragged. And you can find resemblances in the text; the incident with Maritornes, the 'Asturian wench' (III, 2), in *Don Quixote* has resemblances to the farcical bedroom scene at the end of *Joseph Andrews* (but so have many others, see Ehrenpreis's Afterword to the 'Signet' edition of *Joseph Andrews*, p. 304—and why not go back to Chaucer's *Reeve's Tale*?). Don Quixote is an 'everyman'; there is something of him in all of us: a man who loses his ability to see reality and then, when he recovers it, dies. The Spanish knight haunted Fielding's imagination; there is a resemblance to Sancho Panza in Partridge, following Tom Jones across the moonlit country-side as he seeks glorious death in action against the Jacobites. Fielding took the framework of Cervantes's novel, I think, and the gaunt, larger-than-life frame of Don Quixote himself and filled them with his own moral purposes and comic imagina-tion.

3. There was Fielding's classical scholarship, his ambition to write an English 'comic epic poem in prose' in imitation of Homer's lost comic epic, 'The Margites' (which means 'The Booby'). For this see Fielding's own preface to *Joseph Andrews*. This, a carefully worked out 'statement of intention' before the first important modern novel, should be an important document, but somehow isn't. The real attempt at an epic came seven years later, with *Tom Jones*. To the modern reader the preface seems to belong to a much older period than the novel, which is so fresh and modern. It certainly does not read, with its laboured definitions of 'the ridiculous' and of burlesque, like an intro-duction to the English novel. Perhaps Fielding wrote it with his tongue in his cheek.

4. There was the Bible. Abraham Adams, journeying through a foreign land 'inhabited only by Jews and Turks', as he once began to suspect, is clearly meant to remind us of his biblical namesake, and so is Joseph, with whom Lady Booby plays the role of Potiphar's wife. There are at least two incidents in the novel with biblical parallels; Joseph and the postilion reminds us of the parable of the Good Samaritan, and Adams nearly loses his

son in an incident which is like a parody of the sacrifice of Abraham and Isaac.

There were other influences, some far from minor ones. Hogarth, for example (see Praz, *The Hero in Eclipse*), may have played a crucial part, enlarging Fielding's moral vision and making the novels possible. And Fielding had other models besides Cervantes. There were the French romances of the previous century, Marivaux, Fénelon—whose *Aventures de Télémaque* (1699) Fielding mentions in his preface. There were the 'picaresque' novels from which *Joseph Andrews* takes its form. The picaresque novel was (literally) a 'rogue's tale', from the Spanish word, *picaro*; its form was usually that of a journey, with an adventure for each chapter—which is the form of *Joseph Andrews*.

And possibly most important of all, if we look at Chapter 1 of the novel we may see hints of another, not so much influence as intention. This is a very short chapter. Having got the preface off his chest, and before he starts on the novel proper, he begins, 'It is a trite but true observation that examples work more forcibly on the mind than precepts . . .', and he goes on to talk of 'best men', and continues, 'In this light I have always regarded those biographers who have recorded the actions of great and worthy persons of both sexes. . . . Such as the history of John the Great, who, by his brave and heroic actions against men of large and athletic bodies, obtained the glorious appellation of the Giant-Killer . . .'

Was Fielding attempting, as others did in this century, to write a novel about a Christian hero? This was the century in which *The Gentleman's Magazine* ran a competition, the object of which was to define the Christian hero. Richardson's third novel, *Sir Charles Grandison* (1753–4), and forgotten novels like Brooke's *The Fool of Quality* (1766–72), which was admired by John Wesley, are on this theme: an attempt to examine and define goodness. Milton, at this time second in influence to Shakespeare among post-classical writers, had chosen for his epic, *Paradise Lost*, not pagan heroes, but the Bible itself.

Before we get too confused with all these possible influences, let us have a separate look at the first one.

Pamela's story is all in Volume One of Richardson's novel. In Volume Two she is married and the drama and tension are over. Volume One begins with the death of the squire's mother. Almost at once Mr. B. lays siege to Pamela, politely, charmingly, but insistently. His housekeeper, Mrs. Jervis, is his agent. He threatens to send her away but keeps putting it off. The drama of the novel is in the atmosphere. One sees nothing of the outside world. One gradually begins to realise that Pamela is not going to get away. Her letters become more agitated; the squire's attentions become more insistent:

> 'Hush!' said I, 'Mrs. Jervis, did you not hear something stir in the closet?'—'No, silly girl,' said she; 'your fears are always awake.'—'But,' said I, 'I think I heard something rustle.'—'May-be,' says she, 'the cat may be got there; but I hear nothing.'
>
> PAMELA 49. Everyman's Ed.

Then Pamela is abducted; she is kept a prisoner in the house. The gentle Mrs. Jervis is replaced by the sinister Mrs. Jewkes. Pamela is offered a mock marriage, which she knows to be false. Her only friend in the outside world other than her parents, who are helpless, is Mr. Williams, the parson, who is, like her, impotent against the absolute power of the squire. Richardson brilliantly exploits the claustrophobic atmosphere. Over a hundred years later Sheridan le Fanu wrote a thriller, *Uncle Silas*, which borrows directly from *Pamela*—as she is hemmed in, bit by bit, by Mr. B. Like the heroines of Fielding her beauty is irresistible but there is no one else to see it. *Pamela* is really an obsessive, terrifying novel.

It is entirely about sex; Pamela's closet, the lust of Mr. B., are at the centre of it. Because all the action is revealed through Pamela's letters, one gets the—unintended—impression that Pamela herself is thinking of nothing but sex. This is a technical problem which Richardson tackled more successfully in his second epistolary novel. Pamela by necessity has to praise herself. As the action proceeds she is beginning to fall in love with the squire and he, while his cruelty to her increases, begins to be ashamed of it. ' " I must tell you," he says to his friend, Mr.

Brooks, when it is all over and they are married, " . . . that her person made me her lover, but her mind made her my wife."' It is unfortunate though that this has to be revealed through the pen of Pamela herself; it suggests a coy insincerity, and this is what Fielding saw in it from the beginning.

Pamela is a novel which Fielding could not have written; he had none of this morbid, prying sensitivity, preoccupation with the minutiae of day-to-day life, which makes Richardson so modern. One can understand without necessarily agreeing with it what Doctor Johnson meant when he said that Richardson knew more about 'nature' than Fielding. But it was the working-out of the novel which really offended Fielding. *Pamela, or Virtue Rewarded* was the title, and for Pamela the rewards of virtue are on this earth, and very material. With her marriage her goodness and her gratefulness become cloying, and the novel becomes an orgy of sweetness. The 18th-century preoccupation with goodness has produced something false and monstrous; Richardson, having built up a powerful head of emotion, indulges in it.

Fielding lacked sensitivity to atmosphere; his writing is intensely masculine. But he recognised this falsity in *Pamela*, an indulgence in emotion for the sake of emotion, which strikes the modern reader as mawkish and sentimental. Here is Pamela, married to Mr. B., attempting to depreciate herself:

> Mr Perry said, 'I never before saw so young a lady shine forth with such graces of mind and person.'—'Alas, Sir,' said I, my master coming up, 'mine is but a borrowed shine, like that of the moon. Here is the sun, to whose fervent glow of generosity I owe all the faint lustre that your goodness is pleased to look upon with so much kind distinction.'   PAMELA 363

As for the seduction scenes, it is Pamela, as Fielding saw it, who seduced the squire. And certainly the two occasions when Mr. B. penetrated into her bedroom, once getting as far as into the bed, Pamela describes with a detail which invites this charge; her 'conspicuous literacy' is a convention, as Richardson intended it, but it falsifies Pamela. Fielding saw that Richardson was 'mad about sex' (to use the words of V. S. Pritchett); that this novel that was raved about as an example to virtuous women was an incitement to any attractive woman to use her virtue to gain material ends. Pamela's virtue, once we put the novel down with its spellbinding qualities, and think about it, is altogether too good to be true. It got under his skin, and he had to do something about it.

'AN APOLOGY FOR THE LIFE OF MRS. SHAMELA ANDREWS'

So he wrote *Shamela* in 1741, a year after *Pamela* and a year after Colley Cibber had published *An Apology for the Life of Mr. Colley Cibber, Comedian*. In this work there had run a rich strain of self-advertisement. Cibber in Fielding's eyes was a buffoon, whose main enemy was the 'English language' which he abused every time he used it. But he was a pretentious and very successful buffoon. In the preface to *Joseph Andrews* Fielding defines his targets as vanity and hypocrisy and goes on to speak of Colley Cibber in the first chapter: 'How artfully doth the former, by insinuating that he *escaped* being promoted to the highest stations in Church and State, teach us a contempt of worldly grandeur!'

Cibber and *Pamela* together—the combination of false modesty and worldly success was overpowering. At this time Fielding was passing through a particularly bad period, short of money, his wife and daughter ill. He sought consolation in his undogmatic Christianity; in 1740 he had published in *The Champion*, which was now defunct, four essays entitled *An Apology for the Clergy*. But here he saw the clergy being deceived *en masse*, so he attacked both targets, by attributing *Shamela* to 'Conny Keyber'.

Shamela is an abridgment, down to details, of *Pamela*. It has Fielding's unmistakable stamp, apart from the details (like the already old-fashioned 'hath' for 'has', for example, which Fielding used). Like Richardson's novel it is in the form of letters. Richardson in his second edition included many commendatory 'puffs' of his novel, so Fielding in *Shamela* does the same. Then begins a letter from Parson Tickletext. He is one of the many clergymen who have been taken in: 'Herewith I transmit to you a copy of sweet, dear, pretty, *Pamela*', he writes to the wiser Parson Oliver, who has in his possession the very different, 'authentic' letters of Shamela, which he then uses to disabuse the naïve Ticklctext. It is the business of Parson Oliver to stand for the best type of clergyman. The parody that follows is bawdily amusing; that it infuriated Richardson we know from his subsequent attitude to Fielding. Shamela is revealed as Fielding saw her, a sham—a self-seeking, vulgar servant-girl. Richardson's characters—and this is significant to the later novel—become types, illustrations of the passion of lust. They are all caricatures; Richardson's anonymous but very real Mr. B. becomes Booby, a name from the comedy of manners, which was a development from the Jonsonian comedy of humour.

He is made a fool of by Shamela, who really lusts all the time after the virile, rubicund parson—in this way Richardson's characters and his story are turned inside out. Williams the parson is, as we might expect, an enthusiastic disciple of Fielding's *bête noir*, the Methodist Whitefield, though it is a caricature of Whitefield's doctrine that he preaches: do what you like, provided you go to church and pray. '*Be not righteous over-much*' (this is aimed also at Shaftesbury, who said that nothing should be excessive, even virtue) is the text of his sermon to the lovers. It contains an echo of Pamela's pretended bewilderment, as Fielding saw it, as she talks rather whiningly about her moral upbringing to Mrs. Jewkes:

'But then, what comes next? Why, it pleases God to take my good lady; and then comes my master: and what says he? Why, in effect it is: 'Be not virtuous, Pamela.'   PAMELA 176

There is a passage in *Pamela* where the squire, now subdued entirely by Pamela and shortly to be married to her, meets Mr. Williams. The parson had been attracted to Pamela and she and Mr. B. knew it. But unlike Mr. B. he had to curb his passion. He had tried his best to help her and as a result had been imprisoned through the act of Mr. B., on the pretext of a sum of money he owed the squire. We see, all in Pamela's words, Pamela and Mr. B. now revelling in their legitimate passion, and Mr. B. graciously forgives the parson and invites him into his coach:

How generous, how noble, was this! Mr. Williams had tears of pleasure in his eyes; I was silent: but Mr. Williams said, 'Sir, I shall be taught by your generosity, to think myself unexcusably wrong, in all that could give you offence; and my future life shall shew my respectful gratitude'. PAMELA 274

Perhaps the most nauseating thing about this is Pamela's self-satisfaction. Later in *Joseph Andrews* Fielding captures this aspect of her character with precision when he makes her join her husband in urging her brother, Joseph Andrews, not to marry Fanny now that he is a gentleman and she, herself, a lady:

> 'Sure, sister, you are not in earnest; I am sure she is your equal, at least.' 'She was my equal,' answered Pamela, 'but I am no longer Pamela Andrews; I am now this gentleman's lady, and, as such, am above her.' IV, 7

But in *Shamela* the satire is cruder and more impatient. Shamela, having thoroughly mastered the ridiculous Booby, gets him out of the coach by putting on a flood of tears and lustfully invites into it the virile Williams.

Shamela has been described as the best parody in the English language. This it may or may not be, but it is worth reading as the link between *Pamela, or Virtue Rewarded* and *The History of the Adventures of Joseph Andrews and His Friend Mr. Abraham Adams . . . Written in imitation of the manner of Cervantes*. It is a pity that editions of *Joseph Andrews* have very rarely included it; for one modern one that does, see the bibliography.

THE OPENING CHAPTERS OF 'JOSEPH ANDREWS'

The book begins, directly linked with Richardson's novel. Pamela and Squire Booby are married now; Pamela's brother, a handsome young footman, is in the service of Sir Thomas Booby. The Boobys have gone to London and here Sir Thomas dies. His wife, Lady Booby, like her counterpart in Richardson, Mr. B., does not waste any time in laying siege to Joseph's virtue. Her waiting-woman, Mrs. Slipslop, also lusts for him. Joseph, though he had fallen for the fashions of London to the extent of altering the cut of his hair, resists them both, and writes to Pamela about his experiences. Torn by alternate lust and anger, Mrs. Slipslop invents a story that he has got Betty, a maid, with child and persuades Lady Booby, likewise in an agony of frustrated passion which is a caricature of Richardson, to throw him out; without livery and almost penniless.

So far it has been in some ways like a continuation of *Shamela*, though not in letters. Pamela has become Joseph; Mr. B., Lady Booby; and direct imitation, indirect parody. The lusts of Lady Booby and Mrs. Slipslop come up against the solid wall of Joseph's virtue and innocence. Joseph's letters to Pamela (if much shorter and more to the point than Pamela's) are couched in a not dissimilar tone of puzzled innocence. And Mrs. Slipslop is a rough parallel to Mrs. Jewkes, including a physical resemblance. Lady Booby remains to the end of the novel a distorted, burlesque female version of Mr. B., torn between lust for Joseph and anger at his resistance, one moment contemplating the extreme course of marriage, the next rejecting it. But she belongs only to the opening and closing chapters of the book. The centre part is dominated by the character of Parson Adams.

Adams has been there from the beginning, a curate in the employ of Sir Thomas and a friend of Joseph. And in Book I, Chapter 11, after Joseph has set out on his adventures, 'in bright moonlight', we learn of the existence of a new character. Joseph (and here the parallel with Richardson ends—Pamela had no boy friend) is in love. He sets out from town to country towards his Fanny and she, we learn later, shortly afterwards sets out to meet him, having heard of his early misfortune on the road.

THE INDEPENDENT DEVELOPMENT OF THE PLOT

The story that follows is the story of a journey, which ends when the author's fund of invention, of new things to be met over the hill, gives out. As in *Don Quixote*, two characters remain with us; others come and go.

There are two major incidents in the journey of Fielding's novel, which come at the beginning and end of it. The first is basically sombre, the last the most farcical and riotous of all Fielding's many riotous scenes. Like the other incidents that come in between, on the surface they appear to be isolated episodes like the rest. And linking the whole succession of incidents, 'stories within stories', is a plot based on mistaken identity. The characters journey blindly and those who have nowhere to go, as Ehrenpreis says, travel farthest. They blunder into one another as they blunder into their adventures; coincidence, or Providence —in fact Fielding himself, as he tells us—looks after them; in the end Joseph and Fanny discover who they really are, and that solves their problems.

THE JOURNEY

Joseph Andrews is a short novel, and the journey can be described briefly if the minor incidents are omitted. Right at the beginning Joseph is set upon by thieves, beaten up and robbed. Lying naked by the roadside, he owes his life to a postilion, 'later transported for robbing a hen-roost', who lends Joseph his greatcoat, in contrast to the selfishness of the other travellers on a passing stage-coach. Meanwhile Parson Adams is travelling from the country to London, where he hopes to sell a volume of sermons. He meets Joseph by accident, recovering from his wounds at an inn, and here discovers also that he has left his sermons behind him. So Adams turns back and he and Joseph, now recovered, set off together.

Their method is what Fielding calls 'ride and tie', sharing one horse between them. The result is they are continually separating. One by one the other characters from the opening chapters overtake them. Fanny, coming in the other direction, is saved by Adams when on the verge of being raped. She then joins them, making three. Both Fanny and Joseph exert a physical charm which is irresistible to any reasonably young person of the opposite sex whom they meet. Adams for his part will get into a passionate discussion which, unless interrupted, will be followed by violence. These simple rules give a 'comic strip' quality to the novel.

In contrast to this are three episodes of a type which belong to those 17th-century French romances, of which Fielding gave a list in the fourth paragraph of his preface. The first, 'The history of Leonora, or the unfortunate jilt', is told by a coach-companion of Mrs. Slipslop and the second, the story of Mr. Wilson, is at the centre of the journey and of the novel, while the third, 'The history of two friends', awkwardly brought in near the end, is left unfinished.

Up to this point, from the moment that Joseph set out from London, the plot has been the journey. There has been no development, just a series of disconnected events, apparently, in which everything happens by accident. But now they have reached the Booby estate which is everybody's destination and, first at Adams's house and then at the Booby house, it is quickly worked out.

Mr. Booby and Pamela have joined the other characters. Lady Booby is trying to prevent the marriage of Joseph and Fanny and gets them arrested on a trumped-up charge, but Squire Booby intervenes to save his future brother-in-law. Fanny is nearly raped for the third time; a new character, a city fop, Beau Didapper, tries to seduce her. A pedlar, who has made one brief earlier appearance, turns up at the Adams house and provides the first stage of the dénouement: Fanny, he reveals, was kidnapped by gypsies and is really Pamela's sister and therefore Joseph is her brother.

The action then moves to Lady Booby's house. Here, that evening, occurs the comic bedroom-scene, beginning with Beau Didapper seeking Fanny's bed and finding instead Mrs. Slipslop, and ending with Adams waking up in the same bed as Fanny, discovered there by Joseph. The following morning Mr. Wilson, the character from the central episode, comes on a promised visit and it turns out that Joseph is his son, and was substituted by gypsies for Fanny when they stole her from the Andrews parents. So Joseph and Fanny are now once more free to marry and furthermore are both of the same social rank—Fanny through her relationship to Pamela. Lady Booby is powerless to prevent their marriage. Everybody is happy who deserves to be happy and Lady Booby soon finds a 'young captain of dragoons'.

FIELDING'S INTENTIONS

Did Fielding start off with the intention of writing a second parody of Richardson and change his mind?

I don't think he did, for the following reasons. First of all, the material was just not there. Pamela being slowly, yard-by-yard, room-by-room, enclosed and assaulted by Mr. B., is one thing, Joseph receiving the same treatment from Lady Booby is another. It was the age of the 'double standard'; men were not expected to behave according to the moral code they allotted to women. It could be argued that this was part of the joke, but it is just not a long enough joke to sustain a novel, and Fielding, I believe, knew it; he shows it by the speed with which he gets through what one might call the 'Richardson' material. Joseph has resisted both Lady Booby and Mrs. Slipslop by Chapter 11 and is off on his travels. He shows it also by the lack of any attempt to portray Lady Booby (or Joseph) in depth, in the sort of depth Richardson portrayed Pamela and Mr. B. But this may have been, it could be argued, due to Fielding's limitations.

Doctor Johnson said to Boswell, 'I indeed, never read *Joseph Andrews*'. But some of the things he said about Fielding have more application to *Joseph Andrews*, it seems to me, than to the two novels of Fielding he did read, *Tom Jones* and *Amelia*. Richardson, Johnson said, 'enlarged the knowledge of human nature and taught the passions to move at the command of virtue'. Comparing Richardson and Fielding, he said that there was 'all the difference between the characters of nature and the characters of manners; and *there* is the difference between the characters of Fielding and those of Richardson'. Richardson was 'a man who knew how a watch was made', against Fielding, 'who could tell the hour by looking at the dial-plate'.

I think there is a real, important distinction here; Johnson, though unfair, is right. Fielding's characters are from the theatre, from the 'comedy of manners'; they are theatrical caricatures. The theatre invited caricature; Shakespeare, who imitated 'nature', was in this unlike that other Elizabethan dramatist, Ben Jonson. The 'comedy of manners' is a development from the earlier 'comedy of humour', such as those plays by Jonson (*The Alchemist*, *Volpone* and others) in which each character represents a 'humour', or a passion in its extreme form, and the 'natural' characters tend to be flat and negative. Fielding says in his preface, 'I might observe that our Ben Jonson, who of all men understood the ridiculous the best, hath chiefly used the hypocritical affectation'—and the hypocritical affectation also preoccupied Fielding.

The division that Doctor Johnson pointed out persisted far into the history of the English novel; between those who described 'nature' (like Jane Austen, who may have learnt from Fielding, but whom Dr. Leavis prefers primarily to link with Richardson), and those who describe 'manners'. Fielding and Smollett inaugurated a literature of caricature, 'flat' characters, characters, as E. M. Forster describes them in his *Aspects of the Novel*, who can be expressed by one sentence ('I will never desert Mr. Micawber'); who are in fact incapable of really changing or surprising us. In fact, Johnson and Fielding said virtually the same thing about characters. In *Joseph Andrews* (III, 1) Fielding said, 'I declare here once for all I describe not men, but manners; not an individual, but a species.' This anticipates the words of Imlac, from Johnson's *Rasselas*, quoted in Chapter 2 of this book. Fielding goes on:

> Perhaps it will be answered, Are not the characters then taken from life? To which I answer in the affirmative; nay, I believe I might aver, that I have writ little more than I have seen. The lawyer is not only alive, but hath been so these four thousand years; and I hope G—— will indulge his life as many yet to come.

Fielding wanted his characters to be universals, which was why he did not imitate reality with the dogged persistence of Richardson. He was interested in the whole sweep of society, life itself; he did not have Richardson's relentless, probing curiosity into one particular human situation.

So, as in *Shamela*, which is about 17,000 words in length, Fielding's treatment of Richardson's theme is self-destructive. From the beginning the solid characters of Richardson have become flat, theatrical sketches. The dialogue is brilliant, in a theatrical way:

> 'I am sorry for it' cries Slipslop, 'and if I had known you would have punished the poor lad so severely you should never have heard a particle of the matter. Here's a fuss indeed about nothing.' 'Nothing!' returned my lady. 'Do you think I will countenance

lewdness in my house?' 'If you will turn away every footman,' said Slipslop, 'that is a lover of the sport, you must soon open the coach door yourself, or get a set of mophrodites to wait upon you, and I am sure I hated the sight of them even singing in an opera.' 'Do as I bid you,' says my lady, 'and don't shock my ears with your beastly language.' 'Marry-come-up,' cries Slipslop, 'people's ears are sometimes the nicest part about them.'   I, 9

One gets the impression in these opening scenes of impatience, of something being got through quickly. This is the Fielding of the theatre, writing his plays on the back of 'tobacco-paper'. One can hear the laughs from the gallery at lines like Lady Booby's: 'Do you think I will countenance lewdness in my house?' and Mrs. Slipslop's mispronunciations anticipate Mrs. Malaprop in Sheridan's *The Rivals* of a generation later. The names themselves, of course, Slipslop, Booby, are from the comedy of manners; in contrast to the biblical ring of Joseph Andrews and Abraham Adams.

Joseph Andrews has its own strengths, which Richardson's novel did not possess. Joseph stands for 'purity . . . male chastity' (I, 1, closing lines), and you might detect a note of irony here. But Fielding was not being ironical when he said, to summarise the opening paragraphs of this chapter, that his intention was to write a book about a Christian hero, or when he described Adams in his preface as his most outstanding and original character ('. . . as it is the most glaring in the whole, so I conceive it is not to be found in any book now extant'). Adams, he hoped, 'will excuse me to the gentlemen of his cloth'. Adams is at the centre of the book, and I think Fielding intended this from the first. Middleton Murry considered that Adams and Lady Booby are the two 'most real' characters in the book. As for Richardson's *Pamela*, it is the supreme example of what Fielding referred to in his preface as 'the true ridiculous': 'the ridiculous only, as I have before said, falls within my province in the present work.'

I should add that most authorities, for example *The Cambridge History of English Literature*, take the view that Fielding started with one intention and changed his mind in mid-stream. You will have to make up your own mind.

6

'Joseph Andrews': 2. Characters, Themes

PARSON ADAMS

Tickletext and Williams in *Shamela*, and the five other clergymen who make their brief appearances in *Joseph Andrews*, illustrate in their different ways weaknesses of the church in Fielding's time. Clergymen swarm in Fielding's novels; only Trollope, among major novelists, was more interested in them. If we don't see them directly they are lurking in the background; for example, Mrs. Slipslop was 'the daughter of a curate'. Generally their status (like that of the schoolteacher today) was uncertain if not depressed; socially they were on the defensive (Adams and Trulliber come to mind), they could easily slip right down to the bottom ranks of society. Adams had the salary of a manual worker; but he, among them all, was the good man, like the Poor Parson in Chaucer's *Canterbury Tales*.

Goodness is the most difficult thing to portray because, in fiction if not in life, it tends to be negative, like white paint. Colonel Dobbin in Thackeray's *Vanity Fair* may owe a lot to Adams; looking for other 'good' men and women in literature, we might think of some of the minor characters in Dickens, such as the Peggottys. The achievement in the case of Adams is that his goodness is made into a positive quality. From the time that a 'grave person' enters the inn where Joseph is lying, we begin to feel this goodness as a force. The 'good' characters in fiction, if they are alive at all and yet not sentimentalised and sweetened like Richardson's Pamela, tend often to be so because of some incidental eccentricities of character, and Adams has been said to be like this, just a bundle of external characteristics, made out of 'pipe, crabstick, snapping fingers and Aeschylus'.

I don't think this is true. Adams is not a flat character; he is always capable of surprising us. Take the very end, for example, where he is discovered by Joseph in bed with Fanny. Can we predict how he will react in this embarrassing situation? I don't think so. Fielding is supposed to have based Adams on a real, very eccentric character whom he was friendly with, the Reverend William Young, and Adams to the last is a living person, entirely convincing and never the mere 'luminous disc of a pre-arranged size', as E. M. Forster described flat characters. Not in the least embarrassed, Adams blames the situation on witchcraft; and a moment later, his mistake having been explained to him by Joseph, he is striding about the room, still in his shirt, 'rubbing his hands', apologetic and delighted at the same time by the explanation, in words that link up with *Pamela*:

> He then traversed the room, rubbing his hands, and begged Fanny's pardon, assuring her he did not know whether she was man or woman.   IV, 14

Here are Richardson's words:

> 'Sir,' said I, 'that was very bad: and it was too plain you had the worst designs.'—'When,' said he, 'I tell you the truth in one instance, you may believe me in the other. I know not, I declare (beyond this lovely bosom), your sex; . . .'   PAMELA 181

'Goodness' was the preoccupation of the time; here we have Fielding's against Richardson's. The absolute power of the squires, so often abused, excited writers from the time of Addison's Sir Roger de Coverley with the idea of portraying power and benevolence combined, but Fielding saw when he was writing *Joseph Andrews* (though maybe not so clearly when he created Allworthy in *Tom Jones*) that goodness does not go well with temporal power. Adams has an income of £23 a year, compared with the £20,000 that Peter Pounce, Lady Booby's steward, has casually acquired. In the novel he is always without funds, so always at the mercy, in one sense, of the people he meets—though his expectations at every new encounter are always high. Like Shaftesbury, he is an optimist, and his assumption that everybody he meets will be as generous and good-hearted as he is is matched only by his fury—if anybody under his protection, such as Fanny or Joseph, is involved—when he finds they aren't. Don Quixote expected giants and robbers as Adams expects goodness in human nature.

But he has no understanding of it; he 'never saw further into people than they desired to let him' (II, 10). What he does possess is Shaftesbury's 'moral sense': 'which apprehends the rightness or wrongness of actions without recourse to reasoning'. Adams is the true 'man of feeling'—which became the title of a popular novel by Henry Mackenzie in 1771; his feelings are always sound He passes through the novel as though *he* (not it) is a test: you can judge characters by the way they react to Adams. Parson Barnabas ringing the bell 'with all the violence imaginable' to get away from him; those that try to make fun of him, like the doctor (I, 14) or, more brutally, like the young squire (III, 7), only reveal themselves. In the face of that sort of thing Adams behaves with composure; Lady Booby's furious reaction to his decision to marry the two lovers despite her opposition shows him at his most impressive, in his moral strength, against her great temporal power:

'Madam', answered Adams, 'I know not what your ladyship means by the terms master and service. I am in the service of a Master who will never discard me for doing my duty; and if the doctor (for indeed I have never been able to pay for a licence) thinks proper to turn me from my cure, God will provide me, I hope, another.'

IV, 2

It is against lack of charity, meanness of spirit, or brutal manners to a third party, that he shows his anger. His frequent involvement in physical violence is the more comic because he is by nature pacific. But when emotion takes charge of him—despite his own advice to Joseph (IV, 8): '"No, Joseph, do not give too much way to thy passions, if thou dost expect happiness."'—it overwhelms reason, the 'judgement' which Locke demanded. There might even have been physical violence against Mrs. Slipslop if a coachman hadn't interrupted her, in Book II, Chapter 13. Adams 'took two or three strides across the room'.

He does this too as Wilson unfolds his tale of moral deterioration and debauchery in London:

> '... In a word, I debauched her.' (At which words Adams started up, fetched three strides across the room, and then replaced himself in his chair.)　　　　　　　　　　　　　　　　　　　　　　　III, 3

We see Adams vividly in details like this; we feel his generous anger. Possibly this sort of behaviour was Fielding's, because Tom Jones, otherwise so different, does just the same, listening to the confessions of the Man of the Hill:

> 'I believe it from my soul,' cries Jones, 'and I pity you from the bottom of my heart.' He then took two or three disorderly turns about the room, and at last begged pardon and flung himself into his chair, crying, 'I thank heaven I have escaped that.'　　VIII, 11

The scenes of 'low life', those scenes which Fielding's critics found offensively vulgar, usually have Adams at their centre. Covered with hog's blood, blackened by a mop, in the wrong bed: 'A dreadful quarrel', reads the chapter heading, imitating Cervantes, 'with its bloody consequences to Mr. Adams.' But Adams is not just a figure of knock-about farce, a Punch-and-Judy doll. One can underestimate Adams because the externals are always so vivid. One sees his goodness in scenes like the following, when Joseph and Fanny come together for the first time:

> If prudes are offended at the lusciousness of this picture, they may take their eyes off from it and survey Parson Adams dancing about the room in a rapture of joy. Some philosophers may perhaps doubt whether he was not the happiest of the three, for the goodness of his heart enjoyed the blessings which were exulting in the breasts of both the other two, together with his own. But we shall leave such disquisitions, as too deep for us, to those who are building some favourite hypothesis, which they will refuse no metaphysical rubbish to erect and support; for our part, we give it clearly on the side of Joseph, whose happiness was not only greater than the parson's but of longer duration; for, as soon as the first tumults of Adams's rapture were over, he cast his eyes towards the fire, where Aeschylus lay expiring, and immediately rescued the poor remains,

to wit, the sheepskin covering, of his dear friend, which was the work of his own hands and had been his inseparable companion for upwards of thirty years.   II, 12

This is a dramatisation of selflessness. Theatrical, like so many of Fielding's most effective incidents, it is in this case possibly more effective described than on the stage. Like so much of Fielding the action is clothed in a plethora of words, but skilfully. It might have been a weakness that he sees it necessary to mention Adams's 'goodness of heart'. When authors have to tell their readers how good their characters are it is very likely because they are at a loss for ways of showing it otherwise, but this alternate revealing, describing, discussing, is part of Fielding's method; you have to accept it if you accept Fielding. The 'philosophical disquisitions' expand into a bubble of words destroyed suddenly by the single word, 'rubbish'; and this prepares us for the simplicity of what follows. Adams's reaction is not described and we feel it the more acutely.

Adams has his faults. Humourless, prosy, vain, he has no ability to gauge the person he is talking to; to adapt himself to his surroundings. He has no knowledge of the world—he assumes naïvely his sermons will be a gold-mine. He is taken in by everybody he meets. He thinks himself the greatest of all schoolmasters. But his scholarly vanity is endearing because it is so unselfconscious, as, for example, in this small incident from the 'trial' of Adams and Fanny:

> Adams could hold no longer. 'Friend,' said he, 'I have a boy not above eight years old who would instruct thee that the last verse runs thus: "Ut sunt Divorum, Mars, Bacchus, Apollo, Virorum."' 'I'll hold thee a guinea of that,' said the wit, throwing the money on the table. 'And I'll go your halves,' cries the other. 'Done,' answered Adams . . .   II, 11

Of course he has no money in his pocket, which completes the comedy of the incident; the worldly dignity of Adams is always being punctured. But like his shabby, ridiculous appearance, which Fielding seems to go out of his way to draw attention to, it makes his real, moral dignity the greater. The one scene which has an explicit biblical reference, when his son is nearly sacrificed, may be an example also of irony at the expense of Shaftesbury. In his *Characteristics* Shaftesbury says:

> But it is necessary to remark, that even as to kindness and love of the most natural sort (such as that of any creature for its offspring) if it be immoderate and beyond a certain degree it is undoubtedly vicious. For this overtenderness destroys the effect of love, and excessive pity renders us incapable of giving succour.   I, 250

Belief in moderation was also Fielding's philosophy, but immoderate 'kindness and love' is difficult for him to stomach. Amid prolonged, prosy theorising Adams says:

> 'All passions are criminal in their excess; and even love itself, if it is not subservient to our duty, may render us blind to it. Had Abraham so loved his son Isaac, as to refuse the sacrifice required, is there any of us who would not condemn him?'   IV, 8

Then he hears news that his son is drowned, and gives a demonstration of that very 'excess' which he condemned. Fielding never took Shaftesbury too seriously.

Fielding enjoys bringing out the grotesqueness of Adams's appearance:

> It is not perhaps easy to describe the figure of Adams; he had risen in such a hurry, that he had on neither breeches, garters, nor stockings; nor had he taken from his head a red spotted handkerchief, which by night bound his wig, turned inside out, around his head. He had on his torn cassock, and his great-coat; but as the remainder of his cassock hung down below his great-coat; so did a small stripe of white, or rather whitish linen, appear below that . . .   III, 12

It contrasts with the neatness and sophistication of men like Beau Didapper, just as Didapper's small frame is contrasted with the sturdy limbs of Joseph. Adams, wading carelessly through water when there is a path alongside, or sitting on a stile, oblivious of his surroundings, to read his Aeschylus, belongs to the country, as do Fanny and Joseph. The dichotomy of town versus country is central to *Joseph Andrews* and *Tom Jones*. The town—and here is the relevance of the central episode, Mr. Wilson's story—is corrupt, sophisticated, hypocritical; the country is Shaftesbury's 'nature'; evil is there too but in this idyllic setting it becomes part of the 'universal harmony'; Shaftesbury's God, 'best natur'd one in the World', is in His Heaven and we always know that Fanny's latest would-be ravisher will be thwarted.

JOSEPH, FANNY, LADY BOOBY

Joseph develops as his journey proceeds. The young man who 'scraped an acquaintance with his parti-coloured brethren' on his arrival in London, went abroad in the morning with his hair in papers, and is nonplussed by Lady Booby's advances, grows up to lecture Adams on the merits of public schools. He hasn't got Adams's larger-than-life, archetypal quality; the biblical overtones are there to be found, but don't thrust themselves forward. We are reminded constantly of Joseph's physical beauty and manliness, as if he were a 'comic-strip' hero. He is a preparation for Tom Jones, but unlike Jones he is perfect, and therefore not very real.

Fanny herself is very much a 'comic-strip' character, I think. She and Joseph owe their uncomplicated integrity to their country background; in contrast to those town-bred characters such as Leonora, or the youthful Mr. Wilson. They both show resemblances to Pamela in the insistence on physical beauty and, quite apart from Fielding's own preoccupation with this as he lost his own health and good looks, there seems to be an echo of Pamela's ever-insistent 'whiteness'; for example in Betty's observation of Joseph's 'extreme whiteness of his skin, and the softness of his hands' (I, 15). And Joseph's chastity, in the face of Betty as well as all the others, seems somewhat over-emphasised: 'Joseph, in great confusion, leapt from her' (I, 18). We never quite forget that he is Pamela's brother.

Fanny is Pamela as Fielding would have made her, frankly described as a sexual object:

> Her teeth were white, but not exactly even ... Her complexion was fair, a little injured by the sun, but overspread with such a bloom that the finest ladies would have exchanged all their white for it; add to these, a countenance in which, though she was extremely

73

bashful, a sensibility appeared almost incredible, and a sweetness, whenever she smiled, beyond either imitation or description. II, 12 Clearly he has in mind her country upbringing. He goes on to pay tribute to her 'natural gentility' but it is as a luscious sexual object that Fanny appears through the course of the novel, tempting everyone, travellers, squires, justices, fops, manservants, to seduce or rape her. She speaks very little; either she 'rent the air with her cries' (III, 9), or, when danger is over, smiled, 'her bright eyes shining through her tears' (IV, 5). Her one impulsive, independent action is to abandon 'the cow she was milking' to set out after Joseph, when she heard he had been attacked and beaten by highwaymen. In this novel Fielding yearns for Arcadian qualities; Joseph's sturdy limbs are contrasted with those of city fops as Fanny's complexion is compared with the white faces of town ladies. She is the simplest and most innocent of his heroines.

Lady Booby's appearance is left to the reader's imagination; what we get, at length, are her words and thoughts. Fanny, of humble birth, had a 'natural gentility'; Lady Booby is spoilt by her absolute power. This theme—the corrupting effect of 'unconditional and therefore irresponsible' authority, to quote V. S. Pritchett, is seen very vividly in Lady Booby's efforts to thwart the marriage of Joseph and Fanny. The theme is at the centre of Richardson's novel but Richardson does not seem wholly to disapprove of it. Lady Booby, like Mr. B., can almost do what she wants. The one thing she can't do is marry Joseph. Her long agony of mind is exhaustively described. Here is the whole gamut of the passions; pride followed by contempt, disdain, hatred of Joseph, revenge. She gives way as does Mrs. Slipslop to a foolish hatred of Fanny. There is a good little scene between her and her lawyer, Scout, who, as he flatters and panders to her, she promotes from Mr. Scout to 'dear Mr. Scout' and finally to 'good Mr. Scout'. Having given way to her passion for Joseph she is at the absolute mercy of her emotions. There is a moment of irony in Fielding's description of her agony, when she attempts to summon to her aid the power of reason, which Locke recommended:

'Whither did I suffer this improper, this mad passion to hurry me, only by neglecting to summon the aids of reason to my assistance? Reason, which hath now set before me my desires in their proper colours, and immediately helped me to expel them. Yes, I thank Heaven and my pride, I have now perfectly conquered this unworthy passion; and if there was no obstacle in its way, my pride would disdain any pleasures which could be the consequence of so base, so mean, so vulgar—'   IV, 13

She is interrupted in this victory by the news that Joseph and Fanny are brother and sister, which is enough to overturn 'reason' again.

Lady Booby suffers more acutely than anyone else in this book but one feels no sympathy for her. Her meanness of spirit is total. We get one glimpse of what she was like in the old days:

'No, Slipslop, all the time I cohabited with him, he never obtained even a kiss from me, without my expressing reluctance in the granting it.'   IV, 6

THE MINOR CHARACTERS

Mrs. Slipslop, because less powerful, is less revolting than Lady Booby. Her lust for Joseph is not formidable, merely pathetic, and her repulsive appearance prepares her for the more comic role she plays in the bedroom scene at the end. Some people would say there is a hint of cruelty as well as coarseness in Fielding's description of her in Book I, Chapter 6. She is an object, like Smollett's Lismahago in *Humphry Clinker*. Like a wooden doll, she can be knocked about. These minor characters are types; 'species, not individuals', as Fielding says. But they are also Hogarthian; you'll see Mrs. Slipslop in many a Hogarth drawing, and as Fielding said in his preface, Hogarth was a realist, not a caricaturist; he did not exaggerate.

The best of them show a close, careful observation of behaviour which is Hogarthian; for example Peter Pounce, who with the insecure power of the newly-rich, invites Adams into his coach to experience the delight of patronising him and to find out what Adams thinks of him, and admits cautiously to a 'disposition' to charity. Less vivid is the 'gentleman' whom Adams meets (II, 8), who has disinherited his nephew for not going out to the Spanish War and subsequently proves himself to be a notable coward, or the squire who 'promised more than he fulfilled'. These just don't come off, like photographs that fail to take. One of the most successful is Parson Trulliber, a brilliant example of the sort of character who can be summed up by a phrase. His might be: ' "I caaled vurst" ' (II, 14), which he says indignantly to his wife as she is about to serve ale to Adams. Any further information after this one meeting could only blur the clear impression we have of him, with his enthusiasm for his pigs, his domestic authority and ponderous self-importance:

> 'Yes, Sir, yes,' says Adams; 'I have a horse, but I have left him behind me.' 'I am glad to hear you have one,' says Trulliber; 'for I assure you I don't love to see clergymen on foot; it is not seemly, nor suiting the dignity of the cloth.'
>
> II, 14

These are 'types' from the comedy of manners; there can be no development of them. Bearing in mind Doctor Johnson's distinction between Richardson and Fielding; that one describes 'nature', the other 'manners', it is worth comparing one of Fielding's physical descriptions with a similar one by Richardson. Here is Richardson's Mrs. Jewkes (described, of course, by the pen of Pamela):

> Now I will give you a picture of this wretch. She is a broad, squat, pursy, *fat thing*, quite ugly, if any thing human can be so called; about forty years old. She has a huge head, and an arm as thick as my waist, I believe. Her nose is flat and crooked, and her brows grow down over her eyes; a dead, spiteful, grey, goggling eye, to be sure she has; and her face flat and broad: and as to colour, looks as if it had been pickled a month in saltpetre: I dare say she drinks.
>
> PAMELA 97

This is living, incomplete, a first impression that will develop. In Richardson we always see one character through the eyes of another, it is all subjective, there is never any final impression. Contrast with this Fielding's Mrs. Tow-wouse, the innkeeper's wife:

Her person was short, thin, and crooked. Her forehead projected in the middle, and thence descended in a declivity to the top of her nose, which was sharp and red, and would have hung over her lips, had not nature turned up the end of it. Her lips were two bits of skin, which, whenever she spoke, she drew together in a purse. Her chin was peaked; and at the upper end of that skin, which composed her cheeks, stood two bones, that almost hid a pair of small red eyes. Add to this a voice most wonderfully adapted to the sentiments it was to convey, being both loud and hoarse.   I, 14

So with Mrs. Slipslop: 'She was a maiden gentlewoman of about forty-five years of age who, having made a small slip in her youth, had continued a good maid ever since' (I, 6); or Joseph: 'He was of the highest degree of middle stature . . .' etc. (I, 8). This is completed action in the past; and Mrs. Tow-wouse, like Smollett's caricatures, is an object; no longer developing or changing.

This is part of Fielding's technique. He admits, in the words of Henry James, speaking of Trollope, 'a terrible crime . . . that the events he narrates have not really happened'. Fielding makes no effort at all to create a 'suspension of disbelief'; the atmosphere is of a clubroom, Fielding telling a story. As he talks we see the characters, but they are in the distance. We don't breathe down their necks as we breathe down the neck of Pamela, while she sits writing, waiting for Mr. B. to make his next move.

But if we lose by this, we also gain. We see the characters in their context; not only their social context but their moral context. Fielding tells us what he thinks about them, what they think about each other, and in this way we get a picture of society which is wider, more comprehensive, than that of a writer like Richardson who works all the time inside the minds of his characters.

SATIRE

The great weakness and strength of Fielding's novels is that everything happens for a reason. For the more unreasonable, equivocal workings-out of real life Fielding had no time. Providence takes care of everything. He is at his most unconvincing when he is reaching out for coincidences, gypsies and such-like, to bring his characters together and solve their problems. But in *Joseph Andrews* it is the journey that matters, not the destination, and the best passages are those in which moral purpose or comic invention act as a binding force; in the best of them every inciddent, every detail, contributes to the total effect.

In perhaps his most effective piece of satire, at the beginning of the journey, Joseph Andrews, naked in a ditch, is seen by a passing stage-coach:

> Though there were several great-coats about the coach, it was not easy to get over this difficulty which Joseph had started. The two gentlemen complained they were cold, and could not spare a rag, the man of wit saying with a laugh, that charity began at home; and the coachman, who had two great-coats spread under him, refused to lend either, lest they should be made bloody; the lady's footman desired to be excused for the same reason, which the lady herself, notwithstanding her abhorrence of a naked man, approved; and it is more than probable poor Joseph, who obstinately adhered to his modest resolution, must have perished, unless the postilion (a lad who hath since been transported for robbing a henroost) had voluntarily stripped off a great-coat, his only garment, at the same time swearing a great oath (for which he was rebuked by the passengers), 'That he would rather ride in his shirt all his life, than suffer a fellow-creature to lie in so miserable a condition'.   I, 12

Generally Fielding was too interested in life, too much a novelist, to follow through his satire with the remorseless objectivity of Swift. Swift would take an idea and work it out, with an intellectual power matched only by his contempt for the human species. Fielding could never have invented the Yahoos, Swift's savage, bestial 'men', in a world of civilised horses, in *Gulliver's Travels*; his fantasies, such as his *Journey from this World to the Next*, lack power as they move further away from direct observation of life. But in this scene and the ones that follow at the inn, Fielding has a counterpart to Swift's disgust, and that is the intensity of his own reaction to meanness and lack of charity. Fielding really hated meanness of spirit as Swift hated the physical side of *homo sapiens*. One notices in this passage how the greatest irony is enclosed, as if by afterthought, in a parenthesis. The coach moves on, and each of the travellers, lady, lawyer, wit, coachman, behaves according to his allotted role. When they are in turn stopped by one of the robbers and themselves robbed, the affected modesty of the lady contrasts with the elaborately lewd jokes of the lawyer. You feel the latter's nervousness, after the poor exhibition he put up before the highwayman, revealing itself in incessant, jabbering talk: 'an inundation of the like gibberish, which he continued to vent till the coach arrived at an inn'. And you see the lady exactly, when the 'Hungary-water', as she said it should have been, turns out to be brandy, and she 'assured the company (it) was the mistake of her maid'. I think it would be difficult to find another passage in which the second-rateness of a small group of people is more relentlessly displayed. Its biblical parallel is the parable of the Good Samaritan: 'And who is my neighbour?' Fielding asks, like 'a certain lawyer' in St. Luke, Chapter 10. This is the opposite of inflated, burlesque diction, which he promises in his preface; it is understatement, as in Swift.

The satire is usually directed against some form of the arrogant abuse of power: the petty power of innkeepers, or the greater power of squires and justices. The justice who tries Adams and Fanny is in a hurry. The scene progressively builds up from the swift reversal at its beginning, when Adams and Fanny are themselves accused of what they have successfully prevented. This might seem too contrived, were it not for the many incidental details, the confused but always authentic background. At first this background is the group of 'bird-batters', who have taken charge of Fanny and Adams, arguing over their share of the £80 reward. Gradually the throng swells, the voices grow more confused. Fielding is adept at portraying this kind of confusion, mixed motives cancelling each other out, till at length Providence intervenes. There is (see the preface) no major vice; chaotic as the situation is, nobody is particularly responsible, and it is just this that gives a nightmare quality to the scene. The justice is clearly going through a routine. This has happened before; it will happen again. There is no inflation, no exaggeration, the characters reveal themselves. 'Human nature', petty in detail, is collectively vile, and exposed with a quiet savagery worthy of Swift. The discovery of Adams's book of Aeschylus produces the inevitable; it is 'cyphers', a plot against the government. But nobody bothers very much. Fielding captures that hurried, yet casual, confused cross-talk; all courtrooms have something of it:

> The parson taking up the book, and putting on his spectacles and gravity together, muttered some words to himself, and then pronounced aloud: 'Aye, indeed, it is a Greek manuscript; a very fine piece of antiquity. I make no doubt but it was stolen from the same clergyman from whom the rogue took the cassock.' 'What did the rascal mean by his Aeschylus?' says the justice. 'Pooh!' answered the doctor, with a contemptuous grin, 'do you think that fellow knows anything of his book? Aeschylus! ho! ho! I see now what it is ...' ... 'Aye, what's your name?' says the justice to Adams; who answered, 'It is Aeschylus, and I will maintain it.' 'Oh! it is,' says the justice: 'make Mr. Aeschylus his mittimus. I will teach you to banter me with a false name.'   II, 11

This, though Adams did not know it, was the end of his ordeal. One of the company was looking 'steadfastly' at him; he was recognised. At once the justice becomes a very ordinary sort of man, not very effective, rather apologetic. Here we have those minor vices which Fielding promises in the preface: 'rather the accidental consequence of some human frailty or foible', and that is the terrifying thing about it:

> 'Nay,' says the justice, 'if he is a gentleman, and you are sure he is innocent, I don't desire to commit him, not I; I will commit the woman by herself, and take your bail for the gentleman: look into the book, clerk, and see how it is to take bail—come—and make the mittimus for the woman as fast as you can.'   II, 11

The fop, Beau Didapper, intended only self-indulgence. They all seek only to fulfil themselves. Nobody in *Joseph Andrews* is totally wicked. But we see in scenes like this that Fielding had no illusion about the universality of 'good nature'. It was rare.

The practical joking of the young squire and his entourage (III, 7) is not so successful; it goes on too long. Fielding is most successful as a satirist when he models himself on Swift, and leaves verbal inflation for understatement. Adams's story of his life, related to the 'gentleman' (II, 8), is Swiftian in style. The political corruption is revealed the more effectively because it is told with resignation, casually.

HUMOUR

The bedroom scene at the end of the novel is a preparation, as is so much of *Joseph Andrews*, for *Tom Jones*; it has its parallel in the scenes at the inn at Upton, in *Tom Jones*. But the Upton scenes are basically serious, whereas the succession of comic incidents piled on one another in *Joseph Andrews* is pure farce, though Homeric in scale. The scene, contained in not much more than two thousand words, repays detailed examination. Each character re-enacts the role he plays in the novel. It is Didapper's fate not to get his woman, Mrs. Slipslop's to lust unsatisfied—the moment when, her surprise over, she begins to move 'with much courtesy' across the bed towards Adams and is foiled for the second time within minutes is one of those delicious details in which Fielding excels. It is the fate of Lady Booby to come too late and misunderstand, Adams to rush to the help of a woman in distress and cause worse confusion, Fanny to see her virtue in apparent extreme danger. The humour is not mere slapstick, as it is sometimes elsewhere in the novel; always it is true to character. To take one detail, Adams's error in confusing Mrs. Slipslop and Didapper:

> He made directly to the bed in the dark, where laying hold of the beau's skin (for Slipslop had torn his shirt almost off), and finding his skin extremely soft, and hearing him in a low voice begging Slipslop to let him go, he no longer doubted but this was the young woman in danger of ravishing, and immediately falling on the bed, and laying hold on Slipslop's chin, where he found a rough beard, his belief was confirmed . . .   IV, 14

The burlesque is not in the diction here; the language is clear, exact, matter-of-fact, and it would be difficult to find its parallel anywhere for density of comic invention, and sustained, accurate motivation. If Fielding owes his technique to the stage, this is scarcely performable on the stage. Fielding in fact has transformed his theatrical expertise into something new, which we are to meet again, many times, in Dickens, Thackeray, Wells, and thousands of lesser writers. His strength—this comes out clearly here—lay not in imitation of Johnson's 'nature' but in his artistry; because the scene, brilliant as it is, is artificial.

In contrast to this is the mock high-flown language which Fielding likes to indulge in, the mock imitation of the classics, which he refers to in his preface when he says, 'In the diction, I think, burlesque itself may sometimes be admitted'. Here we are at the beginnings of that most tiresome type of humour, the use of long words to describe simple things, which has persisted into this century, dying its slow death in the pages of *Punch* and similar magazines. Fielding was writing a 'comic prose epic', like Homer's lost *Margites*:

> He did not therefore want the entreaties of the poor wretch to assist her; but, lifting up his crab-stick, he immediately levelled a blow at that part of the ravisher's head, where, according to the opinion of the ancients, the brains of some persons are deposited, and which he had undoubtedly let forth, had not Nature (who, as wise men have observed, equips all creatures with what is most expedient for them) taken a provident care (as she always doth with those she intends for encounters) to make this part of the head three times as thick as those of ordinary men . . .   II, 9

The justification for this sort of sentence, which carries on for as long again, is that Fielding is enjoying himself. It is followed by a Homeric simile, interrupting the action: 'As a game-cock, when engaged in amorous toying with a hen . . .' Similarly Homeric is the battle with the hounds:

> Now Thou, whoever Thou art, whether a muse, or by what other name soever Thou choosest to be called, who presidest over biography . . . Thou, who, without the assistance of the least spice of literature, and even against his inclination, hast, in some pages of his book, forced Colley Cibber to write English . . .   (III, 6)

Fielding is skilful in his use of comic bathos, the apparent climax that ends in sudden deflation. One needs to read the whole account of the battle to appreciate to the full the following:

> The parson now faced about, and with his crab-stick felled many to the earth, and scattered others, till he was attacked by Caesar and pulled to the ground. Then Joseph flew to his rescue, and with such might fell on the victor, that, O eternal blot to his name! Caesar ran yelping away. III, 6

The whole Homeric scene, sustained for many hundreds of words, comes crashing down on the one word, 'yelping'.

Fielding is a more subtle humorist than many who have dismissed him as coarse have been prepared to let themselves see. In this novel he is generally—except in that central episode, Mr. Wilson's story—enjoying himself, and the enjoyment reveals itself sometimes in the odd word, or phrase: Parson Adams 'met his son, in a wet condition indeed, but alive and running towards him'—the crisis is over, we can smile. But he shared with Hogarth and many other of his contemporaries a fascinated interest in the grotesque, in physical humiliation. Sexual attraction, which in *Amelia* became heavily charged with guilt, is here either idealised, in the case of Joseph and Fanny, or is good for a joke. With his theatrical experience, his timing is superb. The 'most hideous uproar' which broke out when Mrs. Tow-wouse discovered Betty in bed with her husband ends the succession of events, some comic, some less so, that began with Joseph's robbery; it clears the air as a burst of laughter will clear it, leaving us ready for the next entertainment. This physical humour never becomes nasty or merely scatological because Fielding is so good-humoured, and because he keeps his characters at a distance from him. This is an easy, generous, sunny novel. Vices, he said in his preface, could hardly be kept out, but 'they are never the principal figure at that time on the scene'. Unpleasant characters like the kidnappers of Fanny (III, 9) put their unpleasantness aside in the next chapter and start an argument on what is wrong with the contemporary theatre. *Joseph Andrews* has been often dismissed as just a trial run for the great 'epic', *Tom Jones*. But some people prefer it of the two, for its delightful atmosphere, and for the character of Parson Adams.

THE EPISODES

It has been suggested that the episodes (there are three of them) are 'negative analogues'; that is to say, making negatively the points that the main action makes positively. For example, Leonora, who is everything that Fanny is not, wealthy, sophisticated, clever, nevertheless by trying to be too clever loses both her lovers, while Fanny in her simple tenacity of purpose hangs on to hers.

Certainly the main episode, Mr. Wilson's story, is put deliberately at the centre of the journey. Mr. Wilson's journey, like Joseph's, is from town to country, and we have a picture of the town, described by Wilson, which is very likely autobiographical. The style of this episode anticipates the whole tone of *Amelia*, as does its successor in *Tom Jones*, the story of the Man of the Hill. Fielding, close to his own experience, loses his humour. The satire is sombre and the language, as Wilson's 'rake's progress' gains momentum, takes on the agonised tone of a confessional:

> I fell into the acquaintance of a set of jolly companions, who slept all day, and drank all night; fellows who might rather be said to consume time than to live. Their best conversation was nothing but noise: singing, halloing, wrangling, drinking, toasting, sp—wing, smoking, were the chief ingredients of our entertainment. And yet, bad as they were, they were more tolerable than our graver scenes...
>
> III, 3

It is the tone we shall see later in *Amelia*; 'My happiness consisted entirely in my wife, whom I loved with an inexpressible fondness, which was perfectly returned...' (III, 3).

When the episode is over Fielding returns to the story and gets his characters at arm's length again, and he can see them clearly, laugh at them; but here everything is too close. Mr. Wilson finishes up in the country where he lives happily in retirement from life, like the Man of the Hill in *Tom Jones*. But then into the picture comes the young squire, and casually shoots his daughter's little dog, who dies licking her hand. Arrogance and cruelty have no geographical limits, you can't get away from them. This episode is important, I think, because it shows the basic pessimism that was not far behind Fielding's humour; and it gives an indication of the way in which he was going to develop.

7

'Tom Jones': 1. General Outline, Structure

Tom Jones was written in the years following the '45 Rebellion when Fielding was busy with political journalism and at the same time trying without success to make himself into a barrister, after the death of his first wife. He published it in 1749, seven years after *Joseph Andrews* and two years after Richardson had brought out the first two books of his second novel, *Clarissa Harlowe*. The same year his fortunes finally turned, with his appointment as Bow Street Magistrate. From then onwards law was his chief interest and Fielding became successful, influential, powerful and, to a certain extent, respectable.

GENERAL OUTLINE

You can easily get lost in this enormous (at least by modern standards) and complicated book. Like James Joyce's *Ulysses* it has the advantage from the point of view of the critic of being no chance, inspirational work which defies analysis; on the contrary, if you have the skill and patience you can take it to pieces like a modern aircraft engine.

Tom Jones is in fact the 'comic epic poem in prose' that was promised in the preface to *Joseph Andrews*. It has eighteen books, which is half way between the twenty-four books of Homer's *Iliad* and the twelve books of Virgil's *Aeneid*. This number can then be divided by the reader into three sections of six books each. The first six describe Jones's boyhood. The central six are devoted to the 'journey', which is, significantly, in the opposite direction from Joseph's journey; not from town to country but from country to town. The final six are set in London.

Time, in this meticulously-planned novel, is very important.

Books I-VI cover twenty-one years. You can work out Jones's date of birth as May 1724, because *Tom Jones* is set in the year of crisis, 1745. Politics don't play a very important part in it, but they are used to heighten the tension and to suggest, in the middle 'journey' section, the stirrings of the greater society without. Fielding was a 'public' character and his novels are always public novels; everybody is placed in society, and in *Tom Jones* they are placed in society at a particular time, when the long years of peace and stability gave way to the sort of violence many people half wanted as well as half feared. The England he describes is full of Jacobite sympathisers, innkeepers who are ready to become turncoats, and bands of riotous soldiers. Book VII to Book XVIII covers a period of about six weeks. There are discrepancies. This six-week period begins in late November, though the battle between Jones, Blifil and Thwackum occurs in June. Between that and Jones's expulsion in November from the Allworthy estate (VI, 11) only three weeks seem to elapse—'the late rebellion was at the highest' in November of 1745. For a detailed examination of this see Ehrenpreis's *Tom Jones*. The point is that this sort of thing in a different sort of novel can be as unimportant as, for example, the varying ages of Hamlet, which Shakespeare's audience of course does not notice. But Fielding challenges us to read his novel like a riddle, looking for discrepancies, or clues. 'If the reader will please to refresh his memory by turning to the scene at Upton in the ninth book,' he says (XVIII, 2), 'he will be apt to admire the many strange accidents which unfortunately prevented any interview between Partridge and Mrs. Waters when she spent the whole day there with Mr. Jones.' (Briefly— Partridge and Mrs. Waters had to be kept apart because they were known to each other; Mrs. Waters was Jenny Jones, believed by both Partridge and Jones to be Jones's mother; as it is he finds out who she is some weeks after he has slept with her on one crucial occasion.) This is one of the many things which, had it happened, or had it not happened, would have stopped the novel in mid-career. *Tom Jones* is in this respect like a game of chess, in which Fielding is playing against himself.

The novel is an interlocking pattern of coincidences. Generally it is clear that Fielding planned it, as modern detective stories are planned, to bear this sort of scrutiny. You cheat if you turn to the end. At one point, near the end, he invites us jokingly to believe that Jones will be hanged at Tyburn. We know he won't, but Jones, following the standard pattern of this type of book, blunders from one, apparent, nadir of misfortune to a lower one, becoming more and more hopelessly enmeshed until, suddenly, all is solved. To the reader of 1967, the weakness of *Tom Jones* is quite simply that this is not the pattern of a novel to be taken seriously; it is the 'comic-strip', James Bond pattern. We expect our serious novels, even our serious 'comic' novels, to grow like trees, in which a sort of justice operates throughout—not just at the end. This is the case, broadly, against *Tom Jones*.

BOOKS I–VI: BOYHOOD

Mr. Allworthy of Paradise Hall has come back from a three-months' visit to London to find a baby has been placed in his bed. Jenny Jones confesses, under pressure, to be the mother, but refuses to reveal the father. Later Partridge, the schoolmaster in whose house she has been living, is assumed to be the father and expelled from the estate. Miss Bridget Allworthy, the squire's sister, a spinster of about thirty, takes an immediate fancy to the child, and when she later marries the fortune-hunter, Captain Blifil, and has a child of her own, she openly favours Tom against Master Blifil, which causes the well-meaning Mr. Allworthy to have his first real 'uneasiness' about Jones.

In a succession of carefully-staged incidents, each of mounting importance, Jones's wild, imprudent, passionate 'good nature' is contrasted with the carefully-controlled evil nature of Blifil, as the boys grow up. The atmosphere of these six books is genial, the setting is Somerset, Fielding's birthplace, and the ground covered reminds us repeatedly of *Joseph Andrews*. If there is discord it is against the background of the 'heavenly harmony' (to quote from Dryden's *Ode to St. Cecilia*) of the Fielding countryside. When Jones encounters Molly (V, 10) and leads her into the bushes he is a more human, fallible Joseph Andrews. In these early books Fielding does seem to be under the influence of the genial, optimistic Shaftesbury, the deist—though he is sufficiently objective to make Square, the philosopher, a caricature of the more superficial aspects of deism. These six books and even more the six books that follow are in the pattern of *Joseph Andrews*, the pattern of the picaresque novel: incidents singled out, such as the escape of Sophia's bird (IV, 3), followed by a chorus-like commentary. There follow roadside encounters, adventures in inns, arrogant lawyers and doctors and, in the final section of the novel, amorous, designing 'ladies of quality'. The difference between *Joseph Andrews* and *Tom Jones* is that here everything is more carefully organised. After the apparently haphazard journeying of the earlier book, here everything is for a purpose—though in Books I–VI we are not yet too aware of the machinery of the plot.

What we do begin to realise is that Jones is vulnerable, susceptible to disaster. His early escapades don't do him lasting harm. Feeling himself to be responsible for the discharge of the gamekeeper, Black George, he tries to support this man by secretly selling a Bible and a 'little horse', gifts from Allworthy; when Allworthy discovers Jones's true motive he thinks the better of him for it. Jones is carrying on an affair with Black George's daughter, Molly, and beginning to fall in love with Sophia, daughter of the neighbouring squire. Fielding makes it clear that Molly seduced Jones; Jones 'held it as much incumbent on him to accept a challenge to love, as if it had been a challenge to fight' (XIII, 7). This later becomes his great weakness; he has to learn that in both cases the 'honour' is bogus. Molly becomes pregnant. Jones at once accepts responsibility and hurries to confess to Allworthy, and in the long run this does him no good at all. In fact Molly is probably not pregnant by him; Jones learns this in due course and it helps to 'free' him from Molly, along with a wonderfully comic incident (V, 5) involving Square, the philosopher. Only after this does Jones acknowledge to himself that he is in love with Sophia.

Jones is only too anxious to assume moral responsibility for anything he does, and, whatever he does, his motive is always honourable. And Allworthy seems to realise this; which takes us up to Book V, Chapter 7, when Allworthy falls sick and for a time seems to be dying.

When he recovers, Jones, for a brief period, runs wild. He is in an emotional state, because he loves Allworthy; he is in love with Sophia, and he gets drunk. Dreaming of Sophia, he meets Molly. Fielding knew the relationship between love and lust. 'That hunger', as he describes lust (VI, 1), which 'doth nevertheless seek its own satisfaction as much as the grossest of all our appetites.' The scene that followed no doubt annoyed Doctor Johnson and will always offend people; but that it is 'human nature' there can't be much doubt. Jones is seen by Blifil and Thwackum as he disappears into the bushes with Molly, and rushes from frustrated fornication to aggression. He assaults his schoolmaster and his rival, Blifil.

This is the climax to the first section, and it has an epic quality; Jones, beaten assiduously by Thwackum throughout his boyhood, grows up and beats his schoolmaster, the father-figure. The fascination of these first six books is that the characters are haunting, larger-than-life; they are like the fantastic figures out of a fairy-tale: grotesque, like Thwackum, or ideal, like Allworthy, and the elements of the story have a fabulous (in the original sense of the word), day-dream quality. Jones has achieved manhood. But then comes catastrophe, expulsion from 'Paradise'. Blifil carefully saves up the misadventure and uses it at the right time. In contrast to Jones, who never really knows what he is doing and is a creature of impulse, Blifil is always in control of what he is doing and is particularly a master of timing. Fielding believed that the hypocrite had one big advantage over the honest man; the honest man assumed everybody else to be honest; the hypocrite assumed the reverse, and was cautious. Like the Shakespearean, Machiavellian villain, Blifil is a schemer who keeps winning till he goes too far and over-reaches himself.

Numbed by sudden disaster, Jones sets out with a vague intention of going to sea. He still has a lot to be thankful for; he has Sophia's love, he is young and irresistibly handsome and up to now he has had a lot of good luck. But this sunny, happy atmosphere is not maintained.

Jones decides on second thoughts to join Cumberland's army against the Stuarts. The outside world, which had so far been excluded, begins here to intrude. Sophia also flees, persecuted by her father, Squire Western, because she wants to marry Jones, the bastard, and not Blifil, heir to the rich Allworthy estate. She hopes to find protection from a relative in London.

In this central section the resemblance to *Joseph Andrews* is most obvious. Incidents can be paralleled; Joseph Andrews and Tom Jones both nearly meet a violent death at the beginning of their journeys, after which they recover rapidly despite pessimistic forecasts by casual physicians. The series of events at Upton which is the climax of this section has a parallel in the bedroom farce which comes at the end of *Joseph Andrews*. Parson Adams and Jones both save women from assault in incidents which distinctly resemble each other, and the 'Man of the Hill' is an obvious remodel of Mr. Wilson.

It is in this section, I think, that the reader begins to feel he is being excessively organised. Everybody is on the move now except Allworthy and Blifil; Western has gone in pursuit of his daughter, and a new character, Mrs. Fitzpatrick, comes into the pattern, pursued by her husband, while two characters from the first section, Partridge the schoolmaster and Jenny Jones, reappear disguised. Partridge reveals himself and decides to join Jones, hoping to gain by it in the end, fascinated by Jones and yet fearful, like Sancho Panza joining Don Quixote. Jenny Jones is now Mrs. Waters with a past, and we don't recognise her. Others to enter this concourse of moving people are two companies of soldiers on their way to the war and in the first of these is Ensign Northerton, who seriously injures Jones in a brawl and who is the current lover of Mrs. Waters (whom Jones later rescues from him). The complexity of all this movement has already been illustrated at the beginning of this chapter, and it can be glimpsed at in this quotation from Ehrenpreis's *Tom Jones*:

In the middle of the book, Tom's supposed mother, Jenny Jones, now disguised as Mrs. Waters, has to arrive at Worcester the day after her beloved Ensign Northerton has quarrelled with Tom at the inn on the Gloucester road, because Northerton must start across country with her 'above two hours before day', just in time to meet Tom at dawn near the bottom of Mazard Hill.   IX, 7

But *Tom Jones* is symmetrical. At its exact centre (Books IX and X) occurs the combination of incidents at Upton. Remember that 'Mr. Wilson's story' presided in the same way over *Joseph Andrews*. But the latter episode had no direct connection, whatever its thematic one, with the events of *Joseph Andrews* (though Mr. Wilson was forcibly dragged in at the end); Fielding seemed to feel the need of a tale of this kind somewhere in the comic narrative, like the medieval 'exemplum' or sermon, reminding us that life is not really a frivolous business, so he includes one again in *Tom Jones*—but not this time in the centre. The Man of the Hill belongs to Book VIII, Chapters 10–15, and neatly balancing it, on the other side as it were of the Upton incident, is a second episode, the reminiscences of Mrs. Fitzpatrick.

To take these three incidents in ascending order of importance, Mrs. Fitzpatrick's reminiscences are more lively, closer to real life, than the two minor episodes in *Joseph Andrews*, and furthermore they are woven into the story. Both she and her irascible husband are due to make more, important appearances. The Man of the Hill is a more mysterious, 'Gothic' figure than is Mr. Wilson, and the 'negative analogue' is more clear. While Tom pursues his father (or his parentage), it is the Man of the Hill's father who pursues him; and while Tom's journey is from country to town, his is from town to country. More importantly, the Man of the Hill has given up. After an early life very like Fielding's, alternate study and dissipation, he gives way to misanthropy and hides himself from the world. He knows nothing about recent history, and travel, he tells Jones, is a waste of time. It is Jones, learning from life, who rebukes him for this:

> Indeed, you here fall into an error which, in my little experience, I have observed to be a very common one, by taking the character of mankind from the worst and basest among them . . .   VIII, 15

Between these two episodes Fielding puts the 'Battle of Upton', and the events which follow it. This is the *peripeteia* of Greek tragedy, the moment when the action of the tragedy changes its course. Until this time Jones has been secure in the love of Sophia and she has been following in his tracks. They don't meet at Upton—like Jenny and Partridge they are kept apart— but Sophia discovers he is spending the night with Mrs. Waters and goes off at five in the morning, leaving a muff behind on Jones's bed to tell him what she knows—one of the physical objects which weave their way through this story like the *leitmotif* in a Wagnerian opera. This is Tom's second and real expulsion from paradise. Mrs. Waters, like Molly Seagrim, tempted him and he fell (the temptation scene is described exactly as if it were a battle). For the rest of the story Jones goes in pursuit of Sophia, a pursuit however which grows steadily more hopeless as the misunderstanding between them deepens. This is due to Partridge, who can't stop talking, so that Sophia, who hears from time to time of the progress of the two of them, gets the mistaken impression that Jones, having deceived her, is now loosely boasting of their mutual love. Sophia goes on to London with Mrs. Fitzpatrick, who is her cousin, in the hope that she will receive protection there from her fashionable relative, Lady Bellaston. The section ends when Jones also arrives in London, after a little incident with a highwayman in which he shows his generosity of spirit.

BOOKS XIII–XVIII: LONDON

London is the setting of Fielding's grim, pessimistic, Swiftian satire, *Jonathan Wild*, the setting of his plays, the setting of the two melancholy, guilt-ridden episodes of Mr. Wilson and the Man of the Hill, and the background to most of his third novel, *Amelia*. Here Fielding's high spirits (at any rate in the novels) always seem to desert him, to be replaced by a desire to display his guilt. Most people would agree that this last section is the least successful in the book. The plotting thrusts itself upon us; Fielding's technique is at its most brilliant. He is like a juggler throwing more and more balls in the air and keeping them all going. His main objectives, which the reader sees clearly enough, are to lead Tom Jones convincingly out of the morass he is in and to demonstrate that he has learnt his lesson, has become worthy of Sophia. This he does to a very large extent through the introduction of a new character, Mrs. Miller. She, related to the wife of the highwayman of the previous section, an unfortunate man whom Jones has set on the path to rehabilitation, experiences at first hand his 'goodness of heart' when he mediates between her daughter, Nancy, and a fellow-lodger of Jones, Nightingale. Nancy is pregnant by Nightingale and, thanks to Jones, Nightingale duly marries her.

This is one of several incidents in this London section which show that Jones is becoming a different, more responsible person. But he has meanwhile to experience his third temptation, from Lady Bellaston herself. This is the most sordid of the three; he becomes her 'kept man'. But his only alternative is to starve; his case seems now absolutely hopeless. With charity, and remembering the ease in 18th-century London with which one could fall from riches to poverty of the grimmest kind, one can understand, if not forgive. As for Sophia, she is besieged and nearly raped by Lord Fellamar, a friend of Lady Bellaston, in scenes that are a preparation for *Amelia*. (Fielding liked to prepare and then repeat his material; it could be said that the first two-thirds of *Tom Jones* is a development from *Joseph Andrews*, the last third a preparation for *Amelia*.)

After this Jones goes deeper and deeper into the morass. He can no more keep his affair with Lady Bellaston from Sophia than he could the other two, and when she herself sees a letter he was somewhat foolishly advised to write to Lady Bellaston offering her marriage (the purpose of it was to end the relationship between them), that finally seems to be the end of his relationship with Sophia. Squire Western and his sister are now in London. They have persecuted, bullied and finally imprisoned Sophia (in a way that reminds us of the treatment Clarissa Harlowe receives from her parents) in their efforts to get her to promise to marry Blifil. She refuses to do this, refuses likewise to marry Lord Fellamar as Lady Bellaston suggests, but refuses also to have anything further to do with Jones. They have met once since Upton—briefly and dramatically. This section is full of scenes such as this meeting (XIII, 11) which would be brilliantly effective on the stage. Jones fights a duel with Fitzpatrick and is imprisoned—this also is a misunderstanding, the result of an unfortunate coincidence. The plotting and the complex motivation become feverish, almost overpowering here. But Fielding has not finished. In prison, Jones hears of the true identity of Mrs. Waters, and concludes he has committed incest. And Mr. Allworthy, accompanied by Blifil, has arrived in London.

As the incidents pile up, become more concentrated, highly-organised and theatrical, there is a conspicuous absence of that broad easy humour which illuminated *Joseph Andrews* and the earlier books of *Tom Jones*. The tone is bitter, sour. There is humour, usually to be found in the magnificent dialogue of Squire Western, but it is often savage:

'What's that?' cries Western. 'Murder! Hath he committed a murder, and is there any hopes of seeing him hanged? Tol de rol, tol lol de rol.' Here he fell a-singing and capering about the room.
XVII, 3

But Blifil has over-reached himself. He has been plotting to make sure that Jones would be convicted of the 'murder' of Fitzpatrick (who, however, recovers). He has used as his agent the lawyer, Dowling, who has played a curious, shadowy part in the whole story, making brief appearances from time to time. Dowling is a very Dickensian character. Mrs. Miller is Tom's passionate champion; she has been pleading his case to Allworthy without making any headway, but now suddenly, in Blifil's world, everything falls apart. Dowling had come to see Allworthy when he was sick, bringing the news that his sister, Mrs. Blifil, had died at Salisbury. He had also brought with him a letter from her, confessing that she, not Jenny Jones, was the mother of Tom. We heard something of this letter at the time, and now we hear all about it, and so does Allworthy. Everything spills out, one thing revealing another. Jones's father was a curate she had met briefly, called Summer. She had the boy while

Allworthy was in London; so the first three chapters of Book I fall into place. Blifil of course had concealed the letter. So Tom Jones finds his identity, and with it recovers his position and his reputation and Allworthy's goodwill and, worthy now of Sophia, marries her. In fact he has not so much changed as emerged from a long tunnel of misunderstanding:

> Allworthy stood silent a moment, and then, embracing Jones, he said with tears gushing from his eyes, 'O my child! to what goodness have I been so long blind.'   XVIII, 11

8

'Tom Jones': 2. Characters, Themes

In the first chapter of Book I Fielding introduces his 'bill of fare';
it is to be *Human Nature*. The plain dishes of the country will be
followed, he promises us, by the spiced, exotic dishes of the
city. He quotes Pope (*Essay on Criticism*):

> What oft was thought, but ne'er so well expressed

—a line sometimes taken to epitomise 18th-century poetry:
nothing profound, spiritual, mysterious or irrational. Somerset
Maugham defined greatness in a writer as the ability to 'see
through a brick wall'. Fielding—and this is what the 19th
century had against him—gives the impression of not wanting
to look too far or too deeply. We must, he says (VIII, 1), 'keep
. . . within the rules of probability'. 'The author who will make
me weep, says Horace, must first weep himself' (IX, 1). In a
chapter headed, 'An Essay to prove that an author will write the
better for having some knowledge of the subjects on which he
writes' (XIV, 1), he suggests that 'one reason why many English
writers have totally failed in describing the manners of upper life
may possibly be that in reality they know nothing of it. . . .
Imitation will not do the business. The picture must be after
Nature herself'. As for the exotic dishes:

> In like manner, we shall represent human nature at first to the keen
> appetite of our reader, in that more plain and simple manner in
> which it is found in the country, and shall hereafter hash and ragoo
> it with all the high French and Italian seasoning of affectation and
> vice which courts and cities afford.   I, 1

This is a healthy, extrovert gusto; it doesn't suggest Richardson's morbid probing, or anything very profound, and when the

seasoned dishes come they turn out to be attempted rape, a duel, and incest which turns out to be a false alarm. We feel Fielding's disgust and boredom with these; he says (XIV, 1), 'I will venture to say the highest life is much the dullest, and affords very little humour or entertainment'.

That, briefly, is the case which Dr. Leavis and others have put against Fielding; that he is not interested in complex human behaviour, and his characterisation is obvious. How true is this?

TOM JONES

Tom Jones is innocent—literally. He is 'harmless', and he means well. You will notice that everything he does of any consequence in the early books is commented on, usually at length, by a chorus of observers, with Thwackum and Square at the centre. One of the most interesting examples of this is the incident of Sophia's tame bird (IV, 3). Jones gives it to her; when nobody is looking Blifil releases it. The bird escapes on to a tree. Trying to recapture it, Jones falls into a canal, the bird flies on and is killed, as Blifil coolly later reveals (he alone noticed it), by a 'nasty hawk'. This incident is full of subtleties. Sophia's agitation when Jones falls into the water is a hint to the reader—not yet to herself—of her feelings for Jones. Blifil claims that he wanted to set the bird free. Fielding uses Blifil's specious excuse to make a parody of the sort of argumentation that belonged to the 'age of reason'; Square, Allworthy, Thwackum, an unknown lawyer (who could be Dowling), finally Squire Western, have something to say. Western, who has no brains for this sort of disputation, comes straight to the truth: 'To venture breaking his neck to oblige my girl was a generous-spirited action' (IV, 4).

Later the squire becomes Jones's enemy, but it is for simple, worldly reasons. Jones, an impecunious bastard, wants to marry his daughter, and Western plans for her a worldly marriage with Blifil, heir to a great estate. When the little difficulty of the money is removed, Western turns from savage hatred to genial enthusiasm without the slightest awareness of inconsistency— because to the squire, Jones is 'all right', as we might say today. In Book V, Chapter 11, he jumps to Jones's defence in his fight with

Blifil and Thwackum. Jones is always safe with people who look straight at him, judge him instinctively. Sophia has this instinctive judgement and she falls in love with him.

But the world is complicated and Fielding draws webs of complications over Jones's behaviour. From the beginning we are aware of a mysterious barrier between Jones and the benevolent Allworthy which, surely, shouldn't be with people living in the same household. Mr. Allworthy never looks straight at Jones; he examines him like the headmaster of a very large school, confronted with Jones Minor who, it has been reported, has done something thoroughly unsatisfactory. With Allworthy, Jones is at the mercy of other people—of their reporting of him, and his behaviour. He is eager to rush into blame, accept responsibility, and at first, with the incident of the Bible and the 'little horse' (III, 8-9), he doesn't lose by this trait. He falls in love with Sophia but he still feels responsible for Molly. Fielding treats this with great subtlety, as he does the whole business of Jones's falling in love with Sophia and she with him. It is mostly done in narrative, Fielding talking about the feelings of the two of them as if they were specimens under glass. He says of Jones, 'And to be the author of this highest degree of misery to a human being' (letting down Molly) 'was a thought on which he could not bear to ruminate a single moment' (V, 5). By this time he had entirely succumbed to Sophia's much superior charms: 'The citadel of Jones was now taken by surprise' (V, 4), but not till he heard he was probably not the father of Molly's child was Jones's heart, 'if I may use the metaphor, entirely evacuated, and Sophia took absolute possession of it' (V, 6).

But as the novel proceeds Jones seems to coarsen. After the first six 'boyhood' books, I think Fielding never takes such care again with motivation. One gets the impression of a Hogarthian Rake's Progress—Jones becoming a little coarser, less worried about consequences, each time. The affair with Mrs. Waters is, as it were, the watershed. She challenges him and he, like a man of 'honour', accepts the challenge. As a result of this he has apparently lost Sophia and despair, you could argue, blunts a scrupulous conscience. By the time Lady Bellaston gets hold of him he is moving from one crisis of agony to another. And I think what does irritate us in the later books is Jones's growing helplessness.

Everything goes wrong for him—from Book IV, Chapter 3 (the incident of Sophia's escaped bird), to Book XIII, Chapter 8, when he offers the fifty pounds he has received from Lady Bellaston to Mrs. Miller for her starving cousin, he has a long, bad period, though in this central 'journey' there are episodes which take our mind away from his fortunes, such as those of the puppet-master, and the gypsies. And Jones himself is changing. This change really becomes apparent when Mrs. Miller comes on the scene. Her cousin happens to be married to the highwayman whom Jones has forgiven and helped (XII, 14), and this generosity, disapproved of so strongly by Partridge, starts a chain-reaction which continues now with Mrs. Miller's determined advocacy of Jones. But at the same time his struggles grow more and more like those of a fly in a web. Mrs. Miller's importance here is immense; in the exotic, 'seasoned' atmosphere of the final books she is like a Shakespearean 'outside' character—like Paulina, for example, in *The Winter's Tale*. Jones is in danger of becoming like Captain Booth in *Amelia*; a sort of whipping-block for Fielding's guilt. Mrs. Miller prevents this. The way in which Jones offers the fifty pounds, his first 'wages' from Lady Bellaston, straight to her is superbly timed. It reminds us of Fielding's life: 'Friendship has called for the money—the tax-collector must call again.' This is the side of Jones that Partridge can make no sense of: 'Every parish ought to keep their own poor,' Partridge says to the beggar-man (XII, 4). But instead of being the end of Jones it is the beginning of his recovery. Mrs. Miller's daughter, Nancy, Nightingale, and the two senior Nightingales, form a smaller world within a world, in which this later Jones moves like an angel of justice, and this is the evidence that after Upton he has changed; he is worthy of Sophia at last. (I think we should remember here that his living as 'kept man' with Lady Bellaston, which has offended more people than has the short, sharp affair with Mrs. Waters, has much more justification; that he and Partridge would otherwise have starved.)

But the justice which Jones administers in his new role is not 'strict justice'!

> He then stept into his chair, and proceeded to Lady Dellaston's, greatly exulting in the happiness which he had procured to this poor family; nor could he forbear reflecting, without horror, on the dreadful consequences which must have attended them, had he rather listened to the voice of strict justice than to that of mercy, when he was attacked on the high road.   XIII, 10

Middleton Murry, defending Jones, uses the expression, 'generosity of the body'; rather a Lawrentian phrase, but clear enough to those who have persisted to this point in their reading of Fielding. Dreaming of Sophia, seeing Molly, he thinks any woman is better than none at all—and this psychological truth, which Thackeray, constricted by Victorian morality, envied Fielding's freedom to take up, enlarged the scope of the English novel.

That is one impression of Tom Jones; I don't think it was quite Fielding's intention to produce this impression. Fielding saw Jones, like Parson Adams in a different context, as being essentially a good man. He was good because he had a warm heart, and because intentions, motives, are what count:

> Mr. Jones had somewhat about him, which, though I think writers are not thoroughly agreed in its name, doth certainly inhabit some human breasts; whose use is not so properly to distinguish right from wrong, as to prompt and incite them to the former, and to restrain and withhold them from the latter.   IV, 6

He follows Adams as Fielding's second major attempt to portray a 'good-natured man'. Sophia saw it with her 'instinctive judgement'. Their estrangement is caused by their separation; one feels, in those middle books, that if she had only met Jones things would have quickly sorted themselves out. We know, when Jones gently turns down Mrs. Hunt (XV, 11), that he has learnt his lesson. Allworthy's final, astonished cry had been anticipated by Mrs. Miller: ' "He is the best-natured creature that ever was born." '

If we compare Allworthy to the other characters in *Tom Jones*, we see that he seems to exist in another dimension. He is a god, a *deus ex machina* (like the gods in Greek tragedy who descend to sort out the complications), whose every move is all-powerful. But he never sees the world he inhabits; he uses his reason, like a blind man reaching out. From the beginning his decisions are liable to be misunderstood. His decision to harbour the mysterious infant is interpreted by the villagers as a confession that he is the father of it, taken along with his mild treatment of Jenny Jones. When he is apparently near death his will, revealed by him in faltering voice, provokes Tom to excesses born of gratitude; though with others—this is Fielding at his most acid—the reaction is different:

> 'The servants will find some token to remember me by', his housekeeper, Mrs. Wilkins, repeats indignantly. 'This is my reward for taking his part so often when all the country have cried shame of him, for breeding up his bastard in that manner; but he is going now where he must pay for all.' V, 8

Allworthy's will, drawn up before he was seriously misled about Tom, was a fair one; so it was generally reviled. All the squire's fair actions were reviled by the world, but his important decisions were never fair, or at least never wise. He ruined the innocent Partridge, sheltered Doctor Blifil, then Captain Blifil, gave his approval to a marriage which was to give his sister no pleasure, took into his household two more rogues, Square and Thwackum, gave them absolute power which was only limited, if it was limited, by their own rivalry and personal enmity, expelled Jones, encouraged Blifil's manifestly absurd pretensions to Sophia and so on. It is true that in a dim way he seems to see sometimes what he is doing. He had his 'doubts' about Thwackum. When Doctor Blifil begins a careful softening-up process for his brother's romance he discovers Allworthy has already seen it and decided to accept it because his sister is a spinster, thirty, and seems to want the captain (I, 12). Allworthy's attitude to the proposed marriage of Blifil and Sophia is distinguished by a complete absence of passion. His calm acceptance of the idea irritates the warm-blooded Western (VI, 3), though when Blifil responds in a similarly calm and controlled way, Allworthy is 'not . . . greatly pleased' (VI, 4). Fielding finds it necessary to defend Allworthy here: '. . . for he had possessed much fire in his youth and had married a beautiful woman for love.' You may notice how often Fielding's praise of Allworthy, or tributes to him, are defensive. But eventually Allworthy is 'pretty well satisfied with what Mr. Western and Mr. Blifil told him, and the treaty was now, at the end of two days, concluded' (VI, 6). Always, with Allworthy, it is what somebody 'told him'. But once he has blinded himself to the merits and demerits of Jones and Blifil, he sticks to his self-deception with all the obstinacy of a man determined not to let himself see the truth. He reproves Mrs. Miller for championing Jones:

> 'Upon my word, Mrs. Miller,' said Allworthy, 'I do not take this behaviour of yours to my nephew kindly; and I do assure you, as any reflections which you cast upon him must come only from that wickedest of men, they would only serve, if that were possible, to heighten my resentment against him.'   XVII, 2

The reasoning in this statement is not good reasoning, if one examines it. One is left to assume that Allworthy, in these weeks when Jones has been on his travels, has fallen completely under the spell and into the power of Blifil.

At the end, confronted with Blifil's deception, Allworthy shows one of his rare moments of emotion; he 'started and turned pale' (XVIII, 11); and he decides to punish Blifil as he punished Partridge, Molly Seagrim, and Jones. It is Jones who persuades him (as he did with Molly) to use mercy and Allworthy is astonished. Partridge's tale of woe (XVIII, 6) is the real indictment of the Allworthy system of administering justice. It is interesting that it should be put at this late stage in the novel. But during the final chapters Allworthy seems to be learning a lot.

So we might ask two questions. How far was Fielding critically aware of Allworthy, and how far does Allworthy's weakness become a weakness in the book?

To answer question one, we might look at some of Fielding's remarks about Allworthy. *Tom Jones* is not a book which leaves things unsaid. Everything and everybody is explained, many times. We will notice, I think, that Allworthy is the most praised character in the book. From the name itself, on to his actions, he is praised. He is referred to as 'that good man . . . this worthy man'; we are treated to short digressions '. . . Mr. Allworthy was in reality as great a pattern . . . of true wisdom . . . as he was of goodness' (VI, 3)—a tendency in Fielding, but Allworthy gets more of it, by far, than anybody else. His benevolence is insisted upon, and there are real examples of it, such as his annuity to Mrs. Miller, with regard to which Fielding says, 'He contrived on all occasions to hide his beneficence not only from the world but from the object of it' (XV, 10). There is no doubt that Allworthy's intentions are good; but it is his fate always to be taken by surprise. 'It may be wondered that a story so well known,' Fielding says of Partridge's quarrel with his wife and the rumour that he was the father of Jones, 'and which had furnished so much a matter of conversation, should never have been mentioned to Mr. Allworthy himself, who was perhaps the only person in that country who had never heard of it' (I, 6). He goes on to explain, as always in a defensive way, 'Scandal, therefore, never found any access to his table'. Is Fielding being ironic? Because all the squire's crucial actions are dictated by malicious gossip, or falsehoods maligning the innocent—who are in fact condemned before they can defend themselves. Partridge, Jones, even Mrs. Miller are under threat.

Here is a passage about Allworthy, couched in the tone, half ironic, half defensive, which Fielding so often uses, which suggests Fielding may have been to some extent aware of the weakness of this attempted portrayal of a 'good man':

> . . . for the reader is greatly mistaken if he conceives that Thwackum appeared to Mr. Allworthy in the same light as he doth to him in this history; and he is as much deceived, if he imagines that the most intimate acquaintance which he himself could have had with that divine, would have informed him of those things which we, from our inspiration, are enabled to open and discover. Of readers who,

from such conceits as these, condemn the wisdom and penetration of Mr. Allworthy, I shall not scruple to say that they make a very bad and ungrateful use of that knowledge which we have communicated to them.   III, 5

And after this we are given a rather appalling insight into Allworthy's ideas of how the boys should be educated. He argued on the principle that two bad teachers would cancel each other out: 'He thought, indeed, that the different exuberances of these gentlemen would correct their different imperfections' (III, 5). When Allworthy decides to commit Molly to Bridewell, the House of Correction, Fielding has this to say:

> A lawyer may, perhaps, think Mr. Allworthy exceeded his authority a little in this instance. And, to say the truth, I question, as here was no regular information before him, whether his conduct was strictly regular. However, as his intention was truly upright, he ought to be excused *in foro conscientiae*; since so many arbitrary acts are daily committed by magistrates who have not this excuse to plead for themselves.   IV, 11

'His intention was truly upright'—this is the theme that runs through Fielding's explanations and excuses for Allworthy. Added to this there is another one. He says (II, 6) that Allworthy's 'natural love of justice' was added to 'his coolness of temper'. Allworthy is cold:

> 'Allworthy gave a patient hearing to their invectives, and then answered coldly . . .'   IV, 11

> 'Mr. Allworthy was not one of those men whose hearts flutter at any unexpected and sudden tidings of worldly profit. . . . He received, therefore, Mr. Western's proposal without any visible emotion, or without any alteration of countenance.'   VI, 3

> 'It was Mr. Allworthy's custom never to punish any one, not even to turn away a servant, in a passion.'   VI, 11

Allworthy always behaves coldly, and this is in contrast to Tom, who always, however foolishly, behaves warmly. I don't believe Fielding is being ironic when he calls Allworthy a 'good man', though we know from elsewhere, for example his remarks about Square (V, 5), that when a character knows 'very well how to subdue all appetites and passions', he is not usually approved of by Fielding. No, Allworthy's ultimate goodness is essential to this novel and we must accept it. But he is cold; he lives in a world of abstractions, and because of this he is deceived. Reason, Fielding argues, is no substitute for warmth of heart.

Is Allworthy a weakness in the novel? He is, because he is essentially a 'dead' character. Living in a world of abstractions, he is an abstraction himself. He has no 'instinctive judgement' of the Lockean kind, and only at the end of the book, when at last he sees the real goodness of Tom, does he come to life. No wonder the bad characters scheme and plot so much; at the centre is a man who is as blind as a 20th-century computer. At the end it is relieving to note that, under Tom Jones's care, he is moving into semi-retirement.

SOPHIA

Book IV, Chapter 2, opens with one of the best examples in Fielding of 'burlesque-admitted-to-the-diction'. Like so much in *Tom Jones*, you may feel that it goes on too long. The effect is like a change in a symphony from the minor to the major key; or to use a different image, it is as if the sun has come out. It heralds the advent of Sophia Western:

> Hushed be every ruder breath. May the heathen ruler of the winds confine in iron chains the boisterous limbs of noisy Boreas, and the sharp-pointed nose of bitter-biting Eurus. Do thou, sweet Zephyrus, rising from thy fragrant bed, mount the western sky, and lead on those delicious gales, the charms of which call forth the lovely Flora from her chamber, perfumed with pearly dews, when on the first of June, her birthday, the blooming maid, in loose attire, gently trips it over the verdant mead . . .   IV, 2

The second paragraph concludes:

> . . . bedecked with beauty, youth, sprightliness, innocence, modesty, and tenderness, breathing sweetness from her rosy lips, and darting brightness from her sparkling eyes, the lovely Sophia comes! IV, 2

This is the language of mockery; Fielding is laughing, reminding us of models from the classics and from later romances, keeping emotion firmly at a distance. But Sophia, like Fanny, Mrs. Heartfree (from *Jonathan Wild*) and the later Amelia, is to be a portrait of an ideal. Of these ideal women, Sophia, I think, is the most subtle portrait. Fanny was seen entirely in sexual terms, but when Sophia journeys from inn to inn in the central section of the novel she inspired innkeepers and such not with sexual longing but with respect and awe:

> When that good woman returned, the conversation in the kitchen was all upon the charms of the young lady. There is, indeed, in perfect beauty a power which none almost can withstand; for my landlady, though she was not pleased at the negative given to the supper, declared she had never seen so lovely a creature. X, 3

She is thought to be Jenny Cameron, the mistress of Bonny Prince Charles, because of her extraordinary gentleness and nobility of manner. As Fielding said in his encomium of Sophia (IV, 2): '. . . nor was this beautiful frame disgraced by an inhabitant unworthy of it. Her mind was every way equal to her person.' One remembers Viola's complaint in Shakespeare's *Twelfth Night*:

> And though that nature with a beauteous wall
> Doth oft close in pollution, yet of thee
> I will believe thou hast a mind that suits
> With this thy fair and outward character. I, 2

Saintsbury classed Fielding with Shakespeare as a writer of comedy, and I think that in Sophia we are reminded often of Shakespearean heroines. Fielding had the gift, which the 19th-century novelists did not have, of being able to describe without sentimentality women as seen by man, with those female qualities men dream of rather than see in real life. Though this type of romantically-conceived woman became a trap to Dickens and Thackeray, Sophia is real, and this may be because of Fielding's 'external' technique, and the ironically flippant, burlesque diction, which prevents both Fielding and us from becoming too emotionally involved with her.

Sophia is not so perfect as to be inhuman. She has the sort of human qualities that some of Shakespeare's heroines possess. She can flatter. 'Well, madam,' she says to her aunt, Mrs. Western, who wants her to marry Lord Fellamar, 'and why may not I expect to have a second, perhaps better than this? You are now but a young woman, and I am convinced would not promise to yield to the first lover of fortune, nay, or of title too' (XVII, 4). Mrs. Western has been boasting that she 'had lovers formerly', and this treatment accomplishes its object; the 'evil day' is put off. There is a more subtle passage when Fielding looks into her attitude of mind, faced with the continuous pressure put upon her to marry Blifil:

> The idea, therefore, of the immense happiness she should convey to her father by her consent to this match, made a strong impression on her mind. Again, the extreme piety of such an act of obedience worked very forcibly, as she had a very deep sense of religion. Lastly, when she reflected how much she herself was to suffer, being indeed to become little less than a sacrifice, or a martyr, to filial love and duty, she felt an agreeable tickling in a certain little passion which, though it bears no immediate affinity either to religion or virtue, is often so kind as to lend great assistance in executing the purposes of both.
> VII, 9

Like Rosalind, from *As You Like It*, and Viola, she combines a fresh simplicity of mind with the courage to go out into the world on her own. She has more physical courage than Viola, who trembled at the idea of a duel. 'A good brisk pace,' she says to her maid, Mrs. Honour, 'will preserve us from the cold, and if you cannot defend me from a villain, Honour, I will defend you, for I will take a pistol with me. . . .' (VII, 7). And when a man rides up to her in the darkness (X, 9) 'she neither screamed out nor fainted away'. Sophia, we feel, is generally a more capable character than those other Fielding heroines; she is a squire's daughter, and an heiress. Like Fanny, she has that simplicity which Fielding associates with the country, but it is not a simplicity of mind: '. . . her understanding was of the first rate, but she wanted all that useful art which females convert to so many good purposes in life and which, as it rather arises from the heart than from the head, is often the property of the silliest of women' (VII, 3). Much later in terms of experience, when Lord Fellamar calls on her (XV, 2), she is 'somewhat more a mistress of computation'.

It would be interesting to find a parallel between *Tom Jones* and Richardson's *Clarissa*, in view of the link between the earlier novels of these two. There is the superficial one that each is of epic length, and generally acclaimed its author's masterpiece. I think Fielding could have been influenced by those opening books of *Clarissa* which describe the heroine's persecution by her family. Sophia's persecution by her father and her aunt has many parallels in *Clarissa*. Both Richardson and Fielding seem by 20th-century standards over-anxious to insist on the filial obedience of their heroines, at the expense of the cruelty and tyranny of the parents. Both Clarissa and Sophia promise their parents that they will never marry without permission; both remain passive in the face of mounting cruelty. In Sophia's interminable arguments and pleadings with her aunt there is a strong ring of Richardson:

'Surely,' says Sophia, 'I am born deficient and have not the senses with which other people are blessed; there must be certainly some sense which can relish the delights of sound and show which I have not; for surely mankind would not labour so much nor sacrifice so much for the obtaining, nor would they be so elate and proud with possessing, what appeared to be, as it doth to me, the most insignificant of all trifles.' XVII, 4

The 'trifle' is worldly honour. Sophia has no ambition, except to please her father, '. . . may heaven blast me if there is a misery I would not suffer to preserve you', she says to him (XVI, 2).

Sophia stands out as a contrast to Jones. While he is vulnerable, easily tempted, she is solid as a rock both against alliances with Blifil or Fellamar, pressed by her father and her aunt respectively, and against one with Jones till he proves himself worthy of her. She is not narrow or prudish. She does not hold his sexual freedom against him—she falls in love with him while hearing about it at her father's dinner-table; and Fielding insists that it is Jones's (apparent) making free with her name, up and down the country inns, that offends her. This is important, a touch which shows, I think, Fielding's sensitivity. It would have been beyond Richardson. Sophia gives an impression of moral integrity, more than any other character, I think. She is a woman of principle. In her letter to Jones she says, 'A promise is with me a very sacred thing and to be extended to everything understood from it' (XVI, 5). She, morally, is at the centre, as in the next novel Captain Booth wavers back and forth with Amelia and his home at the centre. No doubt this was autobiographical.

SQUIRE WESTERN

Western is the greatest of Fielding's burlesque characters. Like the caricatures of Dickens he exists in his brilliant dialogue; in this way the dramatist became the novelist. Whenever he talks he comes to life. But he differs from the caricatures of Smollett in that he doesn't remain flat, static. He is always changing, revealing new facets of himself. E. M. Forster said of Dickens's caricatures that their immense vitality suggests 'there may be more in flatness than the severer critics admit' (*Aspects of the Novel*), and Western, even if he is a caricature, is one of the most vital characters in English fiction. What is extraordinary, to me, is that we can dislike him so profoundly, and then love him. In this respect he illustrates Fielding's thesis that men are rarely entirely bad or entirely good. Here, for example, is Western at his worst:

> For this last, and many other good reasons, Western at length heartily hated his wife; and as he never concealed this hatred before her death, so he never forgot it afterwards, but when anything in the least soured him, as a bad scenting day, or a distemper among his hounds, or any other such misfortune, he constantly vented his spleen by invectives against the deceased, saying, 'If my wife was alive now, she would be glad of this.' VII, 4

Sophia had tenderly loved her mother, whom the squire had treated like a 'faithful upper servant'. His treatment of his daughter veers wildly from the maudlin to savage brutality. '. . . Shat ha' un? . . . Shat ha' un?' he shouts at her (XV, 5). After an earlier scene (VI, 7), Jones finds her 'with the tears trickling from her eyes and the blood dripping from her lips'. In contrast to this is his feeble performance before Fellamar's emissary, calling with a challenge to a duel (XVI, 2), or his weak surrender to his sister when she seems in danger of leaving her fortune to somebody else (VII, 5).

But at other times he is delightful. In Book XII, Chapter 2, as he proceeds on the high road after Sophia, he begins to 'bemoan himself most bitterly'. When Parson Supple starts to sympathise he says, 'Pogh! D—n the slut . . . I am lamenting the loss of so fine a morning for hunting.' A few moments later he hears the 'melodious throats' of a pack of hounds and we know he is out of the chase for Sophia and Jones. We love him for his eagerness, his childish impulsiveness. He wants to get on with the marriage as he wants to commit Mrs. Honour to Bridewell for her 'ill-breeding' (VII, 9). His clerk has to dissuade him gently from the latter. There is at least one occasion when he threatens to 'lend a flick', as he puts it, to Allworthy. He has a joy of life which is wonderful on small occasions: 'I can tell you, landlord is a vast comical bitch; you will like un hugely', he says to Allworthy in London, and at moments like this we seem to breathe the spirit of the 18th century. At other times he can be strangely moving:

> Here Blifil sighed bitterly; upon which Western, whose eyes were full of tears at the praise of Sophia, blubbered out, 'Don't be chicken-hearted, for shat ha' her; d—n me, shat ha' her, if she was twenty times as good.'   XVII, 3

Basically, of course, he is weak; as he says revealingly to Allworthy, 'I don't know how 'tis, but d—n me, Allworthy, if you don't make me always do just as you please.'

But we remember him finally from scenes like the following:

> 'D—n me if shat unt. D—n me if shat unt, though dost hang thyself the next morning.' At repeating which words he clinched his fist, knit his brows, bit his lips, and thundered so loud, that the poor afflicted, terrified Sophia sunk trembling into her chair . . .   XVI, 2

Western, like Thwackum, is a demonic character. He is an adult from a child's nightmare, given to elemental fury—'the froth

bursting forth from his lips the moment they were uncorked . . .'
Laughter prevents us from being horrified by him.

BLIFIL

When Blifil is making his awkward advances to Sophia, there is
a resemblance to the repulsive Solmes, in Richardson's *Clarissa*,
though Blifil is a cleverer, more formidable character than
Solmes. There are two interesting things about him. One is that
we never discover his Christian name, and the other is that he is
wholly evil. With regard to the absence of Christian name, this
is surely carrying the 'external' technique to an extreme, unless
we think of him as a return to the older kind of one-name type,
like Bunyan's 'Badman'. His entire lack of redeeming qualities
violates Fielding's general practice and his expressed belief:

> . . . for in this instance life most exactly resembles the stage, since it
> is often the same person who represents the villain and the hero; and
> he who engages your admiration today will probably attract your
> contempt tomorrow.   VII, 1

In one way he is like Allworthy; he is a shadowy figure, an
abstraction, all hypocrisy and egoism. He illustrates Fielding's
view of the peculiar strength of hypocrisy, inasmuch as bad men
expect badness in others and are cautious. His strength is this
wary prudence, in contrast to the wildness of Jones. His weakness,
the corollary to this, is that he assumes that all men are as bad as
he is.

Blifil might have been warned by the fate of his uncle, Doctor
Blifil, who schemed so carefully to get his brother married to
Bridget Allworthy, only then to be superseded by him and
driven out of the estate. Like Allworthy, he uses 'reason', and
like Allworthy, he is an indictment of it. The casual behaviour of
Providence is in the end too much for him. He gets as far as he
does because he makes such careful use of the time factor, and
small details—like adding the 's' on to the 'hares' that Black
George has caught (III, 10). He is adept at these slight alterations.
He is in fact as subtle as Iago, from Shakespeare's *Othello*, and as
with Iago we can only guess at his motivation, other than

jealousy, insecurity and a sense of inferiority—you might say this was quite a lot, but it doesn't totally explain the unrelenting viciousness, though it may make it credible. Blifil knows too much. 'He fancied that he knew Jones to the bottom, and had in reality a great contempt for his understanding for not being attached to his own interest.'

Allworthy's readiness to be taken in by Blifil is the one thing in the novel, like the disguise motif in a Shakespearean comedy, that we have to 'take'; it is really difficult to believe. Mrs. Western says to Lady Bellaston, 'I must do Sophy the justice to confess, this Blifil is but a hideous kind of fellow . . .' (XVI, 8), and with this immediate, 'instinctive' judgement Fielding not only sums up Blifil but unwittingly exposes Allworthy's extraordinary blindness. Though clever, Blifil is not basically, I think, a subtle character—if we except one moment, when he hints at his reasons for wanting to marry Sophia: '. . . he had some further views, from obtaining the absolute possession of her person, which we detest too much even to mention' (VII, 6). In this way Fielding, a straightforward Englishman if ever there was one, shies away from providing one kind, at least, of the sort of 'seasoning' he promised in Book I, Chapter 1.

Blifil generally is an unreal character, an abstraction, like his uncle. I think we really see Blifil alive, as we really see Allworthy alive, only at the end:

> Jones went up to Blifil's room, whom he found in a situation which moved his pity, though it would have raised a less amiable passion in many beholders. He had cast himself on his bed, where he lay abandoning himself to despair, and drowned in tears . . .
>
> XVIII, 11

THEMES

Dr. Leavis said, speaking of Fielding, 'We all know that if we want a more inward interest it is to Richardson we must go'. Fielding insists on keeping his characters at a distance, treating them as objects. This gives him great advantages. He can discuss them, explain what he thinks about them, relate them to religious and philosophical ideas of the time—to the 'elegant Lord Shaftesbury', for example, when Sophia tells a lie (XIII, 12)—and he can shape his incidents to fit his themes.

The trouble is, of course, that the reader is being told too much—at once too much and too little. This is a puzzle, in which what is missed out, is missed out to test your perception. Richardson (or Shakespeare) gives us life. Fielding is telling us what to think.

I think this external, objective method works best with Jones and Sophia. In the case of Sophia, it prevents sentimentality. This brisk approach becomes a barrier against too much emotional involvement. The great emotion that Fielding felt, stemming from his dead wife, he kept, like a good 'Augustan', at arm's length. Control is the essence of classicism, and Fielding followed the classical models.

But in the case of Allworthy and Blifil the method, as I see it, is a failure. There is too much reported speech; too much *information* about them and their thoughts rather than direct showing of them, particularly in the case of Allworthy. Shakespeare (see Iago) would have taken us right into the heart of Blifil. The trouble with Blifil is not that he is (as Iago is) an enigma; he is a sketchy, dim portrait, and so is Allworthy.

As for the minor characters, Partridge, Black George, Thwackum and Square, Mrs. Western, the Fitzpatricks, Fellamar—they must be, to a large extent, types. I think with regard to these characters Fielding's general intentions in the novel, his views about human nature—his themes—are all-important. They are full of interest. Partridge is developing continuously as the novel proceeds; his limitations—a tendency to 'blab', physical cowardice, superstition, vindictiveness and uncharitableness—help to bring out Jones's good qualities. Mrs. Western is an example of the new, politically-minded, intellectual woman whom one sees often in fiction after Fielding, but I know of no 'Mrs. Westerns' before him; he could have been drawing her straight from life (his novel-writing sister, Sarah Fielding, or Lady Mary Wortley Montagu, his cousin?). But it is essential to the external method that only incidents can show characters, and these people who make short appearances just don't do enough to show more about themselves. Their importance in the novel is nearly always a thematic one. They are there for a purpose: the light they throw on the major characters, or on some aspect of human nature.

Take, for example, Black George. Originally Jones is indirectly responsible for his dismissal from Allworthy's employment. So Jones tries to help him. But Blifil, who gave away Black George in the first place, secures his permanent disgrace. Jones then approaches Sophia, in the hope that her father might help him. The position is complicated by this time because Jones thinks he is in love with Black George's daughter, and Sophia is beginning to fall in love with him. So Jones's motives don't look disinterested, but are—in contrast to Blifil's, which appear to Allworthy to be disinterested, and are not. The part that Black George plays in this first, 'boyhood' section is extremely important, because he is the instrument through which Jones shows his 'good nature'; he is never far away, with his nagging wife and his daughters. But we don't learn much about him as a person. We begin to see him as a human being with good and bad in him in Book VI. He is now prosperously employed in the service of Western, thanks to Jones. He feels gratitude to Jones:

> . . . for he bore as much gratitude towards him as he could, and was as honest as men who love money better than any other thing in the universe, generally are.　　　　　　　　　　VI, 12

This sums up Black George. He has just found and appropriated for himself £500 which Allworthy had intended as a parting gift for Jones. Later, in the next chapter, he gets an opportunity to steal a further sixteen guineas. His reasoning here is worth quoting. It shows Fielding's belief that few men are either villains or heroes *in toto*, and it shows the way Fielding treats what we might call the 'stream-of-consciousness' (though described at second hand, not directly) to illustrate ironically, as in Hobbes's doctrine, that reasons are the servants of the desires. When characters argue with themselves, they do so in order to deceive themselves.

> Black George having received the purse, set forward towards the alehouse; but in the way a thought occurred to him, whether he

should not detain this money likewise. His conscience, however, immediately started at this suggestion, and began to upbraid him with ingratitude to his benefactor. To this his avarice answered, That his conscience should have considered the matter before, when he deprived poor Jones of his £500. That having quietly acquiesced in what was of so much greater importance, it was absurd, if not downright hypocrisy, to affect any qualms at this trifle. In return to which, Conscience, like a good lawyer, attempted to distinguish between an absolute breach of trust, as here, where the goods were delivered, and a bare concealment of what was found, as in the former case. Avarice presently treated this with ridicule, called it a distinction without a difference, and absolutely insisted that when once all pretentions of honour and virtue were given up in any one instance, that there was no precedent for resorting to them upon a second occasion. In short, poor Conscience had certainly been defeated in the argument, had not Fear stept in to her assistance, and very strenuously urged that the real distinction between the two actions, did not lie in the different degrees of honour but of safety; for that the secreting the £500 was a matter of very little hazard; whereas the detaining the sixteen guineas was liable to the utmost danger of discovery.

By this friendly aid of Fear, Conscience obtained a complete victory in the mind of Black George, and, after making him a few compliments on his honesty, forced him to deliver the money to Jones.   VI, 13

We next see Black George when he comes to London, now a 'great favourite' of Western, with his master and Sophia. Partridge meets him and recognises him. Black George has not lost his gratitude to Jones; he acts as agent, passing notes between Jones and Sophia, visits Jones in prison and offers him money. Then Fielding makes use of one of his shameless coincidences. Black George has used Mr. Nightingale to invest the £500. Allworthy, going to see his old friend, recognises Black George leaving. He soon discovers what had happened to the £500 he gave Jones, and it is from this time and with this news that his feelings towards Jones seem to begin to change.

With regard to Black George, Allworthy's role is always to punish. Punishing him finally, he speaks of his ingratitude: 'The dishonesty of this fellow I might perhaps have pardoned, but never his ingratitude' (XVIII, 11). Yet it was Black George's gratitude which brought him into the picture again, in Book XV. Black George is an interesting, subtle examination of human motive which is not, I think, excessively cynical. Leavis said, 'Fielding's attitudes, and his concern with human nature, are simple'. I think a distinction has to be made between Fielding's characterisation, which is often simple, and the moral implications, which are far from simple.

A scene which repays analysis, with regard to its moral implications, is 'The adventure of the beggar-man' (XII, 4). Jones meets the beggar-man and gives him a shilling. In gratitude the beggar-man offers to sell him something he has found, which turns out to be a pocket-book with Sophia's name on it—again coincidence is used. In the pocket-book is a bank-note for £100. The beggar-man agrees to lead Jones and Partridge to the spot where he found it. Jones now has a practical reason for following Sophia, and he gives her the money when he meets her (XIII, 11). The beggar-man wants a larger reward; he had had no idea of the value of the note. Understandably, he is cynical about Jones's intentions to give the money to Sophia. Jones asks for his name and address; his 'pure joy and transport' contrasts with the coarser feelings of the beggar-man and Partridge. Partridge would not have given the man a shilling in the first place, and would never have seen the pocket-book. 'There, friend, you are the happiest man alive; I have joined your name to that of an angel,' Jones says to the beggar-man. Partridge wants to beat him because he persists in asking for a share of the money. The incident ends with the beggar-man cursing his parents, who had not taught him to read, when he would have 'known the value of these matters as well as other people'.

Here the 'self-interest', which is so omnipresent in Fielding— see the passage quoted from David Garnett at the beginning of this study—of Partridge and the beggar-man, is contrasted with the motives of Jones. Amongst these, you can find self-interest too. Tom Jones is made up of layers of irony. No characters know what they are doing—what their motives really are. Vice, in

Fielding's view, was present in all classes of society. At one extreme was Black George, at the other, Lord Fellamar. Fielding had no wish to overturn the social order; he criticised the nobility, when he did so, for its failure to lead. Lord Fellamar is not, I think, primarily a satirical portrait. If he is a preparation for the sinister 'lord' in *Amelia*, he has none of the latter's viciousness, and at the end we are left with the impression that he behaved as he did as a result of misinformation.

Lord Fellamar is tainted with the vices of the town. The country, Fielding says, has all the vices of the town: 'The great are deceived if they imagine they have appropriated ambition and vanity to themselves. These notable qualities flourish as notably in a country church and churchyard as in the drawing-room, or in the closet' (IV, 7)—after which comes Molly Seagrim's mock-heroic battle in the churchyard. But *Tom Jones*, taken as a whole, belies these words. You feel Fielding loves his country characters, even Square and Thwackum; you feel he hates, or despises, his town ones. For an example of town life that illustrates this, take Lady Bellaston's 'method' to convince Lord Fellamar of Sophia's attachment to Jones (XV, 3). Sophia's simple warmth of heart makes her stand out in contrast to these cruel, empty people.

JONES, SOPHIA AND THE MUFF

At the centre of the novel is the relationship between Jones and Sophia. The external way he treats this, though it limits him, gives him advantages, not possessed by more 'inward' writers; a classical symmetry, and the ability to use irony with great subtlety. Formal perfection (see Coleridge's comparison of *Tom Jones* to *The Alchemist* and *Oedipus Tyrannus*, quoted at the beginning of this study) is not looked on with much enthusiasm today. But the way in which the muff, as a physical object, is interlocked with the relationship, and then used as a symbol of it, is worth examination.

IV, 3. Escape of Sophia's bird; her 'concern for Jones'.
IV, 5. Sophia's accurate, instinctive judgement of Jones: 'To say the

truth, Sophia, when very young, discerned that Tom, though an idle, thoughtless, rattling rascal, was nobody's enemy but his own'.

IV, 5. Sophia in love with Jones without being aware of it: 'her heart was irretrievably lost before she suspected it was in danger'.

IV, 5. Jones asks a favour of her (he wants her to help Black George). 'She now first felt a sensation to which she had been before a stranger.'

IV, 10. Sophia, 'though I believe she herself scarce yet knew her own intention', nevertheless 'levelled her battery' at him. This metaphor is to be developed later, when Mrs. Waters launches her formidable attack (IX, 5).

IV, 10. Sophia's heart 'discovered the great secret to her'. The squire and Supple are discussing Jones's affair with Molly at the dinner-table.

IV, 12. After hearing more gossip of this from Mrs. Honour, her passion 'became now a scorpion in her bosom'.

IV, 13. The hunting accident. This is central in their mutual falling in love. Jones's bravery made an impression on Sophia and Sophia 'made no less impression on the heart of Jones'. Though he was still involved with Molly, he had 'for some time become sensible of the irresistible power of her charms'.

IV, 14. At this stage the muff makes its appearance. Mrs. Honour tells Sophia that Jones found her muff on a chair, and kissed it, knowing it was hers. This is Sophia's first indication that Jones may love her, as well as Molly Seagrim.

V, 4. Mrs. Honour describes this scene to Jones, and how Sophia has since kept the muff:

> 'Then you told her what I had done?' interrupted Jones. 'If I did, sir,' answered she, 'you need not be angry with me. . . . So to be sure I fetched it her back again, and, I believe, she hath worn it upon her arm almost ever since, and I warrants hath given it many a kiss when nobody hath seen her.'

Sophia and Jones are thus led to each other broadly in the same way that Beatrice and Benedict were pushed into one another's arms in Shakespeare's *Much Ado about Nothing*. But Molly is still in the way.

V, 4. The squire throws the muff up the chimney and Sophia, in

Jones's presence, 'with the utmost eagerness recovered it from the flames'. 'The citadel of Jones was now taken by surprise.'

After this Jones is no longer in love with Molly, but he feels an obligation to her. But then he discovers Square in her bedroom (V, 5), and he hears that 'one Will Barnes, and not himself, had been the first seducer of Molly' and was very likely the father of her child. After this his heart is 'entirely evacuated, and Sophia took absolute possession of it' (V, 6).

But the muff has become the symbol of their relationship, and Fielding continues to use it.

X, 5. Sophia hears of Jones's infidelity with Mrs. Waters and, leaving the inn at Upton, bribes the maid to put the muff, which 'had been the constant companion of Sophia by day and her bed-fellow by night', on Jones's bed, with a note pinned to it on which she wrote her name. In the following chapter, Jones finds it after Partridge has picked it up in the morning from beneath the disarranged bed.

X, 7. Western has arrived at Upton. Jones, distracted, holding the muff in his hand, wanders into the room. Western uses the muff as an excuse to commit him for theft. Mr. Fitzpatrick says 'that stealing a muff was undoubted felony'. But Jones now hangs grimly on to the muff.

XV, 11. The final appearance of the muff justifies also the introduction of Mrs. Hunt. Jones, who was unable to resist Molly, Mrs. Waters or Lady Bellaston, has now enough respon-sibility to decline the offer of Mrs. Hunt. Having done this, he 'went to his scrutoire, took out Miss Western's muff, kissed it several times, and then strutted some turns about his room, with more satisfaction of mind than ever any Irishman felt in carrying off a fortune of fifty-thousand pounds.'

THE COMEDY OF 'TOM JONES'

Tom Jones is a comic novel; we see Fielding's limitations when his characters reach moments of crisis. His technique at moments of agony is to say, as he said of Jones, faced with Sophia's muff: '. . . his thoughts, his looks, his words, his actions, were such as beggar all description' (X, 6). Sometimes it is dramatically effective to draw the curtain on such moments. Book XVIII, Chapter 8, ends dramatically: 'Allworthy then departed, and left Blifil in a situation to be envied only by a man who is just going to be hanged.' But generally he fails in the close examination of any state of crisis. Sometimes he skates over a scene with a few general words: 'It is impossible to conceive a more tender or moving scene than the meeting between uncle and nephew . . .' When he does try to render a serious scene dramatically, too often he becomes merely rhetorical. Here is Squire Western, speaking to his daughter:

> 'I am resolved upon the match, and unless you consent to it, I will not give you a groat, not a single farthing, no, though I saw you expiring with famine in the street, I would not relieve you with a morsel of bread. This is my fixed resolution, and so I leave you to consider on it.' VI, 7

This stilted language was 18th-century 'serious' dialogue up to the time of Sheridan. Compare Jones, speaking to Sophia:

> 'My love I will ever retain, but it shall be in silence; it shall be at a distance from you; it shall be in some foreign land; from whence no voice, no sigh of my despair, shall ever reach and disturb your ears. And when I am dead—' He would have gone on . . . XIII, 11

This is close to the language of burlesque, and Fielding knows it; he punctures it a moment later with Sophia's simple question, 'How he came into that room?'

But *Tom Jones* has density and wide range. I have tried to suggest it is a subtle novel; every time one reads it one encounters new layers of irony. Take, for example, Nightingale's awkward reluctance to give money to Mrs. Miller for her cousin. He wonders if he should, then makes a vague promise; his all-too-human attitude being contrasted with Jones's immediate, positive charity (XIII, 8). Or the release of Nightingale, 'dead drunk', from his uncle's protection, just after this uncle had received news of his own daughter's elopement (XV, 7); in this way one runaway marriage having secured another. *Tom Jones* is like a Dutch painting in which mirrors show further mirrors, taking the picture into greater depths. There are brief, telling pictures of 18th-century life, such as the glimpse of married hatred (VIII, 7): 'Much more she said, but not in his hearing; for having lighted his pipe, he staggered off as fast as he could.' For this sort of thing, no doubt Fielding used material gathered from his travels on the Western Circuit. Much of it is close to the style of journalism inaugurated by Steele and Addison: Partridge, for example, at the theatre (XVI, 5). He sneers at Garrick: 'I am sure if I had seen a ghost, I should have looked in the very same manner, and done just as he did'; and he thinks the King the better actor. '. . . he speaks all his words distinctly, half as loud again as the other. Anybody may see he is an actor.' Or there is the Irishman, never seen again, who 'lay in bed reading one of Mrs. Behn's novels; for he had been instructed by a friend that he would find no more effectual method for recommending himself to the ladies than the improving his understanding, and filling his mind with good literature' (X, 2).

Professor Tillyard (*The epic strain in the English novel*) thought that *Tom Jones* succeeded as a comedy, failed as an epic; Jones (unlike Defoe's Robinson Crusoe) never becomes an 'everyman'; Fielding is genial, remote, not universal. I think that *Tom Jones* is a limited novel. It is like an extended parable. If Fielding did not *know* as much as Richardson, in another way he had greater rightness of judgement. Fielding believed, with Shaftesbury, Pope, and most of his contemporaries, that 'Self-love, the spring of motion, acts the soul'. But that is not to say he is cynical; there is no cynicism in the portraits of Jones and Sophia. The characters are, it is true, always clear-cut and, in this respect, simple; they lack the blurred edges of Richardson, of modern fiction. And the structure of the novel is imposed on them, they don't make the structure. On the other hand, within the structure, they do deserve their destinies; they get their deserts with the help of coincidences which make their own efforts seem ironic. But finally *Tom Jones*, I think, despite its limitations, is a great novel because of the greatness of Fielding himself; his nobility and generosity of mind, and his moral vision are really Shakespearean in quality—even if we admit that in other respects he falls short of Shakespeare.

9

The Other Major Prose Works

'THE LIFE OF MR. JONATHAN WILD THE GREAT' (1743)

Jonathan Wild, the highwayman, was hanged at Tyburn in 1725. He is thought by some to have inspired *The Beggar's Opera* of 1728. Fielding probably worked out his satire in the early seventeen-forties, as he travelled the Western Circuit looking for briefs, and it was published in the third volume of his *Miscellanies*.

In Fielding's satire Jonathan Wild is a power-seeker, like Walpole. His empire is in the underworld, but like Walpole as Fielding saw him he is obsessed by 'greatness', a word which strikes like a hammer-blow at regular intervals through the book. Wild leads a gang, as did the real Wild, based on the receiving and selling of stolen goods (at this time it was almost impossible to bring receivers of stolen goods to justice; Fielding was one of those who helped to change the law). All the major characters in this satire are the vilest wretches, with the exception of a jeweller and his wife, Mr. and Mrs. Heartfree. Wild marries Laetitia Snap, daughter of the keeper of a sponging house, but covets Mrs. Heartfree. He causes Heartfree to be falsely accused of robbery and imprisoned at Newgate and persuades Mrs. Heartfree to fly with him to Holland. Wild is shipwrecked and returns; Mrs. Heartfree has a succession of adventures on foreign shores which we hear about later. In the end Wild, of course, over-reaches himself, and the Heartfrees are united.

The weakness of this satire, to my mind, is that it is too intellectual, too Swiftian. In Fielding's last novel, *Amelia*, there are some magnificently Hogarthian passages of description of the criminal underworld. These are lacking here. Wild is an abstraction. He lectures his gang like a parliamentarian. The argument between Wild and the renegade, Blueskin, reads like a report from Hansard:

> 'Did ever man talk so unreasonably?' cries Wild. 'Are you not respected as a captain by the whole gang since my dubbing you so? But it is the shadow only, it seems; and you will knock a man down for affronting you who calls you captain! Might not a man as reasonably tell a minister of state: Sir, you have given me the shadow only? The ribbon or the bauble that you gave me implies that I have either signalized myself, by some great action, for the benefit and glory of my country, or at least that I am descended from those who have done so.' XIV

There is too much of this. There is very little of the raw life we see in the plays. The Heartfrees are utterly helpless and therefore negative. It is no doubt this, and the general vileness of everybody else, which caused Saintsbury to refer to the 'immense pessimism' of the satire. He rated it higher than *Tom Jones*, which shows how fashions change, and Coleridge thought it comparable with Swift's satires. J. H. Plumb (who wrote a foreword to the American 'Signet' edition) sees the influence of Defoe. For me, the satire leaves no deep impression of pessimism; Fielding does not seem to me to be sufficiently involved. It is a monotonous work saved by moments of humour. Here is Wild, alone in an open boat, engaged in Falstaffian reflections:

> 'What signifies fear? I shall die whether I am afraid or not: who's afraid then, d—n me?' At which words he looked extremely fierce, but recollecting that no one was present to see him, he relaxed a little the terror of his countenance, and, pausing a while, repeated the word, 'D—n!' II, 11

Wild, who is really the most engaging character in the book, then casts himself boldly into the sea. When he is sentenced to death his last act is to pick the pocket of the parson in attendance, he 'applied his hands to the parson's pocket, and emptied it of his bottle-screw, which he carried out of the world in his hand'.

There is one vivid, superbly theatrical passage in the satire. It describes Jonathan and Laetitia in bed together, 'on the morning

of the day fortnight on which his nuptials were celebrated'.
Beginning:

> *Jonathan.* My dear, I wish you would lie a little longer in bed this
> morning.
> *Laetitia.* Indeed I cannot; I am engaged to breakfast with Jack
> Strongbow.   III, 8

it moves step by step into quiet hatred. There is a resemblance to
Sir Peter and Lady Teazle in Sheridan's *School for Scandal* (1777),
though I think there is more strength, certainly more bitterness,
in this passage. It suggests what we may have missed when
Fielding left the theatre.

'AMELIA'

Fielding published *Amelia* in 1751. Of the three novels, it is
obviously the most directly autobiographical. It was his own
favourite, he said later in his *Covent Garden Journal*, when he said
also that he would write no more novels; and it is quite different
from the other two. In many ways it represents an advance.
There is little caricature, no burlesque; it is a serious study of a
group of people, who give the impression of having been taken
straight from life. They have the mixture of good and bad
qualities of real people; in *Tom Jones* Fielding had said most
people were neither villains nor heroes, and here he develops this
thesis.

The theme of the novel is married life, with its temptations and
uncertainties. The background is London, the characters army
officers and their wives and friends—a milieu Fielding knew
well. Amelia is one of his most attractive portraits; ideally con-
ceived, as were her predecessors, faultless as a wife, she yet
manages to be human and always interesting. Her husband,
Captain Booth, is that type of very modern hero, or 'anti-hero',
to whom everything happens. *Amelia* ought to have been a most
interesting novel, and in many ways it is. Though there is none
of the slapstick, the good-humoured bloodthirstiness of the earlier
novels, it is full of dry humour, and the style is no longer so
aggressively 'polished', but plain, unvarnished, wry. It appealed

to some who had disliked the earlier novels; Doctor Johnson read it through 'without stopping'. After a slow beginning it became popular in the 19th century and perhaps Dickens and Thackeray owed more to this work than to the others.

But *Amelia* fails, by general consent today, as a novel. Dr. Leavis said that with *Amelia* Fielding had 'gone soft'. I think there is something wrong with the novel that makes it very difficult to read.

STRUCTURE

Amelia is in twelve books, and the plot, not as complex as that of *Tom Jones*, is crowded with incidents, small developments that very often don't lead anywhere, and episodic material; there are, according to Andrew Wright (*Henry Fielding: Mask and Feast*), twelve such interruptions, increasing as the novel goes on.

At the beginning Captain Booth, arrested for taking an innocent part in a street brawl, is cast into prison by Justice Thrasher, for no other reason than that he has no money. Here he meets some colourful characters, including 'blear-eyed Moll'. Nothing in the rest of the novel is as vivid as these compassionate, restrained, but Hogarthian scenes. And soon he meets an old friend, Miss Matthews, whom he had not seen for eight or nine years. She has been arrested for the murder of Hebbers, her lover, who had been unfaithful to her. She tells him her story, and he in turn describes his runaway marriage with Amelia, and how Doctor Harrison, who is the Allworthy of this novel, looked after his interests, till he went abroad to the siege of Gibraltar. Amelia follows him there, and later they live in France, with his friend, Major Bath and his sister. There is also Sergeant Atkinson, Amelia's devoted foster-brother who has followed Booth overseas to look after him, and Captain James, who later marries Bath's sister, one of the first from whom Booth borrows money. The Booths come back to England after the death of his mother-in-law, and Doctor Harrison sets him up as a farmer. But Booth wants to drive a coach—this is very reminiscent of Fielding's early married life. Soon he is in debt again, and comes to London where he is arrested.

In prison Booth resumes his old relationship with Miss Matthews. Then she is released from prison, bails out Booth, and he rejoins his wife, guilty and profoundly miserable.

But Booth is fond of his wife and their small family, and away from Miss Matthews he is determined to shake her off. She, however, refuses to accept this. Booth becomes terrified that his wife will hear of his adultery. He seeks the advice of Colonel James (as he now is), and it turns out that James is the unsuccessful lover of Miss Matthews who secured her release from prison. He now becomes Miss Matthews's lover, though she still wants Booth. The Booths have little money, no prospects; Booth is pursued by creditors. Their landlady, Mrs. Ellison, has a cousin, a 'lord', who might help Booth to gain promotion. This lord, however, has seen Amelia at the oratorio, and is interested in her.

I think Fielding's intention here is to produce an ironic reversal of situation. Booth, the guilty, adulterous husband, has a wife now threatened by two lovers, whom she, unlike Booth, resists— first the lord, then Colonel James, who is beginning to tire of Miss Matthews. But she dares not tell her husband her fears in case he rushes into a duel; Booth has already fought one duel with the fiery Bath, who 'made no more of cutting the throat of a man upon any of his punctilios than a butcher doth of killing sheep'. Amelia learns from a widow, Mrs. Bennet, who later marries Atkinson, that Mrs. Ellison is nothing less than the pimp of this lord; Mrs. Bennet had been one of his squalid victims. The climax, if it can be called such, the equivalent of the Upton scene in *Tom Jones*, occurs in Book X, Chapter 2. The lord had invited Amelia to a masquerade, as he had invited Mrs. Bennet. Then Colonel James gets tickets for her and Booth. On the advice of Doctor Harrison she stays at home and Mrs. Atkinson, masked, substitutes for her.

But it is a muffled climax. The novel resumes its winding course. Booth is arrested for the third time (Doctor Harrison had procured his arrest earlier, really a misunderstanding), after an interview with Miss Matthews which she had insisted upon, and in which he finally breaks with her. At the bailiff's house he confesses all to his wife, and it turns out she knows already. Then there is the usual happy ending; they come unexpectedly into a comfortable fortune.

Amelia is a difficult novel to summarise because it is so like a piece of real life. For long periods nothing in particular seems to be happening; in fact the novel has a curiously muffled quality. At the beginning the theme is Booth's adultery; for most of the rest of it it is the dangers threatening his wife and the general threat of poverty that hangs over them both.

CHARACTERS, THEMES

Amelia is a model of a wife and mother, all affection, patience, devotion to Booth and the children. But she is lively, she can laugh. There is one moment when she gives up Booth: '. . . your papa is—indeed he is a wicked man—he cares not for any of us' (XI, 9); but this despair does not last long. Generally, she is blind to the faults of her husband.

If the novel is not often read nowadays, it is probably because of Booth. 'Poor Booth'—this is Fielding's adjective—is hopelessly passive. When Trent proposed going to a tavern, 'Booth himself, after some resistance, was at length persuaded to comply'. When Trent (who was an agent employed by the 'lord') proposed a game of cards, 'Booth's consent was obtained, though not without much difficulty'. Booth, blackmailed by Miss Matthews, is off to meet her:

> Booth fetched a deep sigh, and cried, 'How unhappy am I, my dear, that I can't sup with you tonight!' XI, 8

There are plenty of Booths in modern fiction. But Fielding does not seem to have seen Booth objectively. He, more than Amelia, is at the centre of the novel, and he is fundamentally a melancholy, gutless sort of character. (The only critic I have read who has warmly praised Booth, and *Amelia*—'*Amelia* is, just as certainly as *Tom Jones*, a great novel'—is Middleton Murry; he finds Booth a sensitive portrait.)

But *Amelia* is full of incidental felicities. Major Bath is a good satirical portrait, which may well have influenced Smollett's military characters. A giant of a man, his ferocity is matched by his warmth of heart. One has to tread a continuous tight-rope to avoid fighting a duel with him. Booth's turn almost comes early in their relationship when he catches the major 'having on a woman's bedgown and a very dirty flannel nightcap', ministering to his sister, who is ill; Booth rashly says that Bath could not have appeared 'in a situation more becoming his character' (III, 8). For those who like to trace resemblances between Fielding and later novelists, I think there is a resemblance in Mrs. James (Bath's sister) to Mrs. Elton in Jane Austen's *Emma*. Always heralded by 'loud knocking', when she calls on Amelia, she is hard and snobbish, and her husband, Colonel James, matches this with his insensitive, superficial nature. Colonel James is a subtle portrait; Fielding examines carefully his limited qualities:

> In truth, the colonel, though a very generous man, had not the least grain of tenderness in his disposition. His mind was formed of those firm materials of which nature formerly hammered out the Stoic, and upon which the sorrows of no man living could make an impression. A man of this temper, who doth not much value danger, will fight for the person he calls his friend, and the man that hath but little value for his money will give it him; but such friendship is never absolutely to be depended on; for, whenever the favourite passion interposes with it, it is sure to subside and vanish into air. VIII, 5

The Booths, insecure in their poverty, worry about the changing attitudes to them of the colonel and his wife. We get the feel of genteel poverty, of the worry about why one was snubbed in the park. There is a fine, bitter passage of dialogue between Colonel James and his wife (XI, 1), which suggests that Fielding, though he was losing the urge to write fiction, was developing his technique. Miss Matthews hovers on the edge, a lively portrait of a 'demi-mondaine'—like the others, with good in her as well as bad. When she thinks, thanks to her jealous slandering of Booth, that he has been killed in a duel by James, she writes a bitter, honest letter to James; all her actions are conditioned by her love for Booth. Doctor Harrison is more human than Allworthy; he plays with Booth's children and can be waggish with Amelia. There is Atkinson, whose chaste devotion to Amelia, which he reveals at last when he thinks he is dying (XI, 6), is an ironic comment on the adulterous dreams of others.

At times, the novel shades off into the sort of social commentary, half journalism, which Defoe and Addison used to provide. Fielding develops the case against duelling which he touched on in *Tom Jones*. Of the episodes and flash-backs, the histories of Miss Matthews, Booth, Mrs. Bennet, Captain Trent, it might be said in their defence that they support this ruminative flavour in the novel; but the two last, particularly, are rather awkwardly brought in. For long periods the novel just hangs fire; there is too much of: 'From this time to the day of the masquerade nothing happened of consequence enough to have a place in this history'—Fielding's awkward method of bridging gaps which is used in this novel with a persistence that becomes mechanical.

Of the many little incidents, pictures of life, to be found in *Amelia*, my favourite is the incident at Vauxhall, where Amelia and Doctor Harrison are accosted by two young gallants, who treat him with coarse insolence: 'Here's the fellow that eats up the tithe-pig. Don't you see how his mouth waters at her? Where's your slabbering bib?' (IX, 9). They are about to molest Amelia when they are interrupted by Booth and Trent. There is a bitterness in this scene which, I think, is very revealing. Fielding was beginning to dislike the world he lived in. In some ways, *Amelia* might have been written by the 'Man of the Hill' from *Tom Jones*.

WHAT IS WRONG WITH 'AMELIA'?

I think the main thing that is wrong with *Amelia* is Captain Booth. Fielding was writing about himself in Booth; so, perhaps, he was in Jones; but Booth was a side of himself that he couldn't get into perspective. He had tried to use this material in the episodes of the earlier novels, with the same, muffled, 'confessional' effect.

Another weakness, which develops from this, is a negative, misanthropic attitude to life in the novel which seems half-baked; not fully explained or realised. Maybe Fielding was too busy as a magistrate to work it out properly; maybe he was ill; maybe he was just too depressed by the great sea of misery he encountered now in his daily duties—that London poor, on the edge of which Booth, with his little family, hovers: 'They starve and freeze and rot among themselves; they rob and steal and beg among their betters', as he wrote at this time, elsewhere. 'There are more bad people in the world, than good,' Amelia says to her child (IV, 3). In *Amelia*, I think for the only time, Fielding gives way to, and indulges in, the melancholy which hangs at the back of his other writings.

There is a third, structural reason. *Amelia* was planned wrongly. It is both against adultery and about adultery. Book IV, Chapter 1, shows the old, genial, tolerant Fielding:

> Let the reader set before his eyes a fine young woman, in a manner, a first love, conferring obligations and using every art to soften, to allure, to win, and to inflame; let him consider the time and place; let him remember that Mr. Booth was a young fellow in the highest vigour of life; and, lastly, let him add one single circumstance, that the parties were alone together, and then, if he will not acquit the defendant, he must be convicted, for I have nothing more to say in his defence.

But in the next chapter he is talking about 'something outrageously suspicious in the nature of all vice', and this is the tone of the rest of the novel. In the words of Andrew Wright, 'The reader hardly knows how far to condemn Booth for his willingness to respond to Miss Matthews's lures . . . or . . . how far to condone an adventure whose consequences . . . are amusing.' On this score, *Amelia* fails.

'THE JOURNAL OF A VOYAGE TO LISBON' (1755)

In June, 1754, Fielding set out with a party of six, which included his second wife, on a journey to Lisbon in an effort to recover his health. Aix-en-Provence had been suggested, but he was too weak for an overland journey. He kept a diary of it up to the time of his arrival in Portugal, where he died two months later, in October. It was published early the following year and then, after the earthquake in Lisbon, republished in a shorter version.

In all his work the journalist in Fielding is never far from the surface. He likes to talk about life, society, the objects around him; he is interested in reality, never in fantasy. Defoe is the great novelist of this kind of unadorned reality—so much so that one hesitates to use the term 'novel' of even such a work as *Robinson Crusoe*. Fielding shows the influence of Defoe, as well as of Swift, in *Jonathan Wild*, and in his last years, immersed in public life, he seems to have been moving towards this type of writing, away from fiction (we might notice here that Andrew Wright saw Miss Matthews from *Amelia* as a 'kind of waif: a Defoe character in a Fielding world'). The *Journal* is loosely-written, rambling— 'convoluted', as Middleton Murry calls the style—and no wonder. Fielding was dying, from several illnesses, of which his dropsy was perhaps the most tormenting and humiliating. His wife soon began to suffer from toothache, and they were plagued by every conceivable manner of petty problem: delay while waiting for a favourable wind, a rapacious landlady on the south coast, and the arrogant behaviour of Captain Veale, of the *Queen of Portugal*.

While waiting at Ryde for the wind to change they put up with a farmer and his wife, Mr. and Mrs. Francis. Fielding says of Mr. Francis, 'He wished not for anything, thought not of anything; indeed, he scarce did anything or said anything. . . . In a word, so composed, so serene, so placid a countenance, I never saw; and he satisfied himself by answering to every question he was asked: "I don't know anything about it, sir; I leaves all that to my wife."' When Mrs. Francis heard they were coming she washed the house so thoroughly that the whole place was damp, and Mrs. Fielding found a 'dry, warm, oaken-floored barn', to which they retired, to Mrs. Francis's indignant surprise. Her revenge was to charge them up to the hilt for almost nothing at all:

A pennyworth of fire was to-day rated at a shilling, to-morrow at eighteenpence; and if she dressed us two dishes for two shillings on the Saturday, we paid half a crown for the cookery of one on the Sunday; and, whenever she was paid, she never left the room without lamenting the small amount of her bill, saying: 'she knew not how it was that others got their money by gentlefolks, but for her part she had not the art of it.'   237

You may recognise earlier characters in the novels from his description of Mrs. Francis: 'She was a short, squat woman; her head was closely joined to her shoulders, where it was fixed somewhat awry . . .' But Mr. and Mrs. Francis, and the captain, are not caricatures. The general tone of the *Journal* is one of dogged determination to be interested in anything except himself. Occasionally we get glimpses of his suffering. 'Mr. Hunter, the great surgeon and anatomist of Covent Garden' came aboard, 'and, though my belly was not yet very full and tight, let out ten quarts of water'; as a result of this he was 'eased of the great apprehension which I had from the length of the passage'. The last-minute effort to restore his health was doomed to failure, as he moved away from the doctors who knew how to treat him. But to the end he maintained his heroic objectivity, breaking off from the recording of the day's incidents to discuss anything that occurred to him with a sort of desperate eagerness, such as the way a 'few monopolising fishmongers' could defeat the plans of the Westminster market, or the true meaning of the 'strange story of Circe in the Odyssey'. After a row with the captain Fielding threatened to return ashore, but when the captain 'tumbled to his knees':

> I did not suffer a brave man and an old man to remain a moment in this posture, but I immediately forgave him.   270

Fielding was very touchy about his dignity, perhaps because of his second wife's plebeian origin.

Generally, however, the tone of this book is more positive, less pessimistic, than that of *Amelia*. We come closer to Fielding than we do in any of his other writings, maybe; there wasn't time to put up barriers of 'polished' writing. Here, I think, is another, final, authentic glimpse:

> We were seated on the deck, women and all, in the serenest evening that can be imagined. Not a single cloud presented itself to our view, and the sun himself was the only object which engrossed our whole attention. He did indeed set with a majesty which is incapable of

133

description, with which, while the horizon was yet blazing with glory, our eyes were called off to the opposite part to survey the moon, which was then at full, and which in rising presented us with the second object which this world hath offered to our vision. Compared to these the pageantry of theatres, or splendour of courts, are sights almost below the regard of children.   279

There is no such thing, David Garnett said (quoted at the beginning of this study), as 'idealism or poetry' in Fielding. You could say that this is the feverish enthusiasm of a dying man, or that Fielding was developing in new directions too late; that the language is heavy, the description stagey. I think the Fielding you see here is to be found in the earlier work, though he concealed it beneath a flippant manner; 'incapable of description' is a typical Fielding phrase; he knew there was a large area of experience beyond his words.

The diary ceases as Fielding, having set foot in Lisbon, regales himself with a good supper. Seventy-six years later in 1830 a monument was erected on his tomb in Lisbon, on which was written:

Luget Britannia Gremio Non Dari Fovere Natum
(Britain grieves that she is not permitted to cherish to her bosom her native son)

though on the other side further Latin included:

... non quin ipse subinde irretiretur evitandis
(not but that he himself was now and then ensnared by things which he ought to have avoided)

Bibliography

TEXTS

The most comprehensive and recent collection of Fielding is: *The Complete Works*, 16 vols., edited by W. E. Henley (Barnes & Noble, New York, 1967).

Editions published individually are:
Tom Jones, 2 vols. (1962), *Joseph Andrews, Amelia*, 2 vols. (1962), *Jonathan Wild and Journal of a Voyage to Lisbon* (1964) (E. P. Dutton & Co., New York).
Joseh Andrews, Jonathan Wild, Tom Thumb, all published in World's Classics (Oxford Univ. Press, New York).
Tom Jones (Afterword by F. Kermode, 1963), *Joseph Andrews* (Afterword by Irvin Ehrenpreis, 1960), *Amelia, Jonathan Wild* (Foreword by J. H. Plumb, 1961) (New American Library, New York).
Tom Jones, Introduction by R. P. C. Mutter (Penguin Books, Baltimore, Md., 1966).
Joseph Andrews and Shamela, edited by M. C. Battestin (Houghton Mifflin Co., Boston, Mass., 1961).
British Dramatists from Dryden to Sheridan, edited by G. H. Nettleton and A. E. Case, contains the text of *Tom Thumb* with Fielding's notes (Houghton Mifflin Co., Boston, Mass.).

BIOGRAPHIES

W. L. Cross: *The History of Henry Fielding*, 3 vols. (Russell & Russell, New York, 1963).
F. H. Dudden: *Henry Fielding*, 2 vols. (Shoe String Press, Inc., Hamden, Conn.).

M. C. Battestin: *The Moral Basis of Fielding's Art* (Wesleyan Univ. Press, Middletown, Conn., 1959). Primarily a study of Joseph Andrews. Emphasis on philosophical background and on the quality of Fielding's thought.

John Butt: *Fielding, Writers and their Work* (British Book Center, Elmsford, N.Y.). A good introduction to Fielding.

Irvin Ehrenpreis: *Tom Jones* (Barron's Educational Series, Inc., Woodbury, N.Y., 1964). A very scholarly analysis of the novel.

M. Irwin: *Henry Fielding: The Tentative Realist* (Oxford Univ. Press, New York).

Middleton Murry: essay from *Unprofessional Essays* (Cape, 1956). This is a first-class defence of Fielding, against criticism of the previous twenty years.

Andrew Wright: *Henry Fielding: Mask and Feast* (Univ. of Calif., Berkeley, Calif.). A useful general study.

BACKGROUND

(*a*) *Literary*

Walter Allen: *The English Novel* (E. P. Dutton & Co., New York, 1955).

V. S. Pritchett: *The Living Novel* (Random House, New York, 1964).

Ian Watt: *The Rise of the Novel* (Univ. of Calif. Press, Berkeley, Calif., 1957).

(b) *Historical*

Dorothy George: *England in Transition* (Penguin Books, Baltimore, Md.).

G. M. Trevelyan: *Illustrated English Social History*, 3 (David McKay Co., Inc., New York, 1949–52).

(*c*) Philosophical

B. Dobrée: *English Literature in the Early Eighteenth Century, 1700–40* (Oxford Univ. Press, New York, 1959).

B. Willey: *The Eighteenth-century Background* (Columbia Univ. Press, New York, 1941).

General Index

Index to Fielding's Works

Stay On Top of Your Classwork with
ARCO'S 1,000 IDEAS FOR TERM PAPER SERIES

Concise yet thorough guides to the planning and preparation of term papers
for high school and college students—how to plan the paper, how and where
to find research sources, how to organize the project, how to select a topic.
$1.95 each, except where noted.

1,000 IDEAS FOR TERM PAPERS IN:

AMERICAN HISTORY
From pre-revolutionary times to the post-World War II period.

ECONOMICS
From macroeconomic theory to the literature of Smith, Marx, Keynes.

ENGLISH
From Chaucer to modern realism. **1.45**

SOCIAL SCIENCE
Topics on psychology, anthropology, sociology and political science.

SOCIOLOGY
Communications, war, urbanization, family, criminology, research design, analysis of data.

WORLD LITERATURE
From Beowulf to the twentieth century.